GW01606055

Bruin

AND THE RUNAWAY

By Michael Fleet

WAGS Retired Police Dogs, charity supports police dogs from Wiltshire, Avon, Gloucestershire and Somerset and a proportion of the proceeds of all Bruin books will be given to the charity to help with their work.

Illustrations by Claire S Bicknell

Copyright © 2024 by Michael Fleet

All rights reserved. No part of this book may be used or reproduced by any means, graphic, electronic, or mechanical, including photocopying, recording, taping, or by any information storage retrieval system, without the written permission of the publisher Author and Illustrator except in the case of brief quotations embodied in critical articles and reviews.

The rights of Michael Fleet and Claire S Bicknell to be identified as author and illustrator, of this work have been asserted in accordance with the Copyright, Designs and Patents Act 1988.

Please send comments, good or bad,
by email to the author at: bruinstories@gmail.com
For more information Michael Fleet • +44 7836 256693

Illustrator & Designer: Claire S Bicknell: claire@stylographics.com
Bark • Linked in • @101illustrations • +44 7940 599 455

Printed by Palace Printers Cornwall

FSC

Typeset & Designed using DyslexicLogicFont © alice.frendo@hotmail.com
Photography Jack Hudson & David Pimbblet

... Coming soon Book 5

Bruin

• LENDS HIS SUPPORT •

By Michael Fleet

Illustrations by
Claire S Bicknell

Photography © Dave Pimbblet

Dedicated with love to:

Florence, Harriet, Henry and Zoe

This book has been designed for independent readers but can be equally enjoyed by adults, parents and carers alike.

CONTENTS:

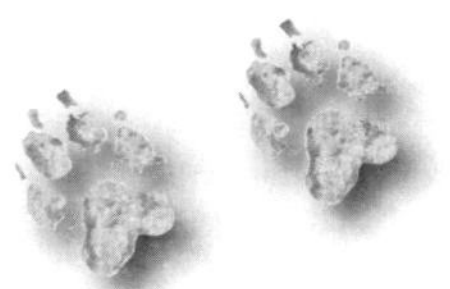

Hearing nothing but the ticking of a clock in the hall she crept downstairs while everyone else was still fast asleep.

Escape from Merrymeet!

Chloe Marsden was 13 years old and was generally a good girl and not used to doing things she shouldn't.

This made her popular at the Merrymeet children's home, not just among the other children but staff as well.

But today was different and the young orphan was about to do the naughtiest thing any child at Merrymeet had ever done.

So, in the darkness of 4am, she pulled on her clothes and sneaked out of her room.

She tiptoed along the corridor and listened for any sounds from inside the peaceful old building.

Hearing nothing but the ticking of a clock in the hall she crept downstairs while everyone else was still fast asleep.

Silently she crossed the hall to reach the front door.

Chloe stopped for a moment to listen again for any noises from upstairs, but everything stayed silent.

So she slowly slid back the bolt, turned the handle and opened the high, wooden door.

There was a chill wind blowing, but Chloe was dressed in her warm fleece jacket and had a rucksack with her important possessions inside.

Keeping as quiet as a mouse she passed through the door and into the chilly outside, feeling a tingle of excitement.

Was she really carrying out her daring plan of running away to join the circus?

She and two others from the children's home had been taken to the circus on Saturday night as a special treat.

And as she watched the exciting acts she thought to herself "that's what I want to do!"

Chloe decided there and then that before the circus packed up and moved off to the next town she would run away and join them.

It was the daring trapeze artists who had really excited Chloe as they flew through the air, as free as a bird.

"I could do that one day," Chloe thought to herself as she looked up at the pair of skillful circus performers.

She knew that it would take years of training to get that good and to start with she would have to do the boring jobs.

But she was willing to take her time and learn.

Before any of that though she had to get away – the lorries taking the big top and all the acts would be leaving that morning which meant it had to be now or never.

So, as the rest of the house stayed fast asleep, she walked quickly and quietly to the pavement outside the Merrymeet Home for Children and headed to the park where the circus had been...

******

Monday morning meant it was a back to school day for the Wilkie children, Florence, Harriet and Henry.

The weekend had been fun, with a family visit to the local aquarium on Saturday morning before Florence and her father had gone to watch Tingleside United in the afternoon.

Harriet had done some baking in the afternoon, making some delicious cheese scones, and Henry had played in the garden with Bruin, their dog.

On Sunday the whole family had taken Bruin for a walk on the beach before going home for tea and Harriet's delicious cheese scones.

But all that was now in the past and a new school week lay ahead. It was business as usual!

On the other side of town it was a quiet Monday morning at Tingleside Police Station and in the dog section there was an air of calmness after a busy weekend.

The three dogs which were part of the first experiment into the police breeding their own animals were all resting at the feet of their trusty handlers.

They were Nelson, his brother Hawk and their sister, Boo, who had all graduated from training with flying colours and were now really useful members of the police dog team.

The youngest of them all (if only by 10 minutes!), their little brother Bruin, had failed the test to become a police dog.

Instead, he had shown himself to be more interested in being friendly and having snoozes rather than controlling crowds or helping to catch criminals.

So that was why he now lived with the Wilkie family as a pet. But even so, Bruin had put his early training to good use.

First he had tracked down Henry after he had wandered off and fallen down a steep bank and then he saved an elderly lady who had been knocked unconscious in a fall at home.

But while Bruin was spending his time as one of the family, Nelson, Boo and Hawk were being kept busy in their jobs with the police.

They had all been used to control rowdy crowds and had also found burglars and other baddies and were keen to do something every day to help keep people safe.

Now, though, it was a quiet Monday morning and the three dogs were just taking it easy.

Nelson was clearly dreaming about earlier action and as he dozed, he made gruff noises as if on patrol and ready for anything.

Suddenly, the calm of the dog unit was shattered

as Nelson let out a loud and bossy bark, followed by some fierce growls even though his eyes remained firmly shut.

"Alright Nelson, pipe down," said PC Gemma Williams, his handler who kept Nelson at home with her in the evenings and made sure he had a warm and comfortable kennel and plenty of good dog food.

Boo and Hawk opened one eye each to make sure nothing was happening. "Oh dear, Nelson's dreaming again about catching baddies," thought Boo before closing her eyes again and catching up with her sleep.

Boo and Nelson had been on patrol on Friday and Saturday night and both had been kept busy so, even if Nelson was having an exciting dream, Boo needed her rest.

Thankfully, peace and quiet soon returned to the dog unit and apart from one more loud, dreamy, bark Nelson didn't disturb the restful atmosphere any more.

Inspector Carlton, the head of the dog unit, put his head around the door and, seeing everyone taking a chance to have a rest, decided to leave them be.

As well as PC Williams, there was Sergeant Ted Ross and PC Gavin Taylor, with Boo looked after by Sgt Ross and Hawk by PC Taylor.

They were all proud of their dogs and, like PC Williams, took them home in the evening and looked after them with great care, while always remembering they were working dogs, not pets like Bruin. The dogs were happy that way and they knew that when the time for action came, they had to be ready.

Bruin, meanwhile, was in his familiar place, dozing in his comfy bed in the kitchen of the Wilkies' house.

On his bed with him were two of his favourite toys, a rubber bone and a knotted, multi coloured rope which Bruin loved to tug on while one of the family held tightly on to the other end.

He was just thinking of his latest walk on the beach when the kitchen door opened and Henry, came in, dressed in his school uniform.

"Morning Bruin," he called out cheerfully as he went to the cupboard to get out a cereal bowl and then a spoon from the drawer.

"Did you have a good sleep?" Henry asked and without looking around or waiting for a reply, which he knew wouldn't be coming, he added: "It's a very chilly morning. I'm going to have Weetabix with warm milk today."

He fetched the cereal from another cupboard and pulled out two of the biscuits to put in his bowl. He was about to go to the fridge for the milk when the door opened again and in came his mummy, in her dressing gown, followed by his sisters Florence and Harriet, both in school uniform.

"Morning Bruin," they each called out in turn but Bruin just carried on lying on his bed, too comfy to bother with getting up, although he did wag his tail.

He loved the family he was living with but he also loved snoozing and he wasn't going to get out of his bed until he really had to.

That was usually after the children went off to school and Mrs Wilkie told him he had to go outside to spend a penny.

Slowly he would sort his legs out so he could get up and then head to the door.

Within a couple of minutes he would be ready to come back in and Mrs Wilkie would have his breakfast ready for him before he went back to his bed.

Mr Wilkie would have arrived in the kitchen before the children went off to school and would have collected the newspaper from the letterbox and be reading that while having his first cup of coffee of the day and tucking into his breakfast.

It was a routine which went the same way every weekday – except during the school holidays.

The next thing to happen would be Mr Wilkie going off to work and then Mrs Wilkie going back upstairs to have a shower and get dressed before starting work on her business.

That was called Happy Cakes, which was making fancy wedding or birthday cakes.

She had a good reputation in the area and people from miles around would be in contact to get special cakes made.

The spring and summer were busiest for wedding cakes but birthday cakes were all year round.

It was now the middle of October and orders were coming in for Mrs Wilkie's very special Christmas cakes and as the weddings slowed down, that part of the business began to get much busier.

But Bruin wasn't troubled by any of that.

He knew that Mrs Wilkie would find time to take him for a walk during the day and once the children were home they would play with him until it got dark.

It was a happy life and Bruin knew that everyone in the family loved him as much as he loved them.

Although he had been bred to be a police dog he just didn't have the heart for it and was put up for adoption, which is how he came to be with the Wilkie family.

He was a pet first and foremost but he was always ready to help if he was needed. That instinct came from his parents, who had both been hard working police dogs.

On this morning, Mrs Wilkie came back into the kitchen and looked at her laptop to see what orders needed working on that day.

"A birthday cake for Jimmy who will be seven, and another one for 18-year-old Paris," she said out loud.

The first cake was to be in the shape of a space rocket and then one made as a horse jumping over a fence, with a girl rider. "She must love horses, this one," said Mrs Wilkie to herself as she began to draw out a design for the cake.

Bruin had gone back to his bed after breakfast and was happily snoozing as Mrs Wilkie got on with her work.

Back at Tingleside Police Station there was at last activity.

A report had come in of an old man who had gone missing that morning from his home in Myrtle Crescent.

The old man was said to be in a confused state and it was very important he was found as soon as possible.

Inspector Carlton came in to the dog unit and announced that they had an urgent job and Sgt Ross and Boo were given the job of helping to track down the missing man.

As Boo was loaded into Sgt Ross's police van, both Nelson and Hawk were looking out of the window and gently whining.

It was as if the dogs could send messages to each other and this one would have been sending good luck wishes to Boo in her task.

"Come on you two," said PC Williams to Hawk and Nelson, getting them to come away from the window and settle back down.

"Boo knows what she's doing and she'll be getting on with the job," PC Williams told them.

Secretly though she wished she had been given the job. She was as keen as the dogs to get out and do some good, rather than sitting in the station waiting for some action.

But for now, that was what she had to do! 

PC Richards put an arm on her shoulder and told her: "I'm sure it will be alright now we've got Boo on the case," he said.

Find Mr Jenkins

Boo and Sgt Ross pulled up outside a bungalow in Myrtle Crescent. A police officer was already there talking to an elderly woman who had a worried look on her face and who kept tugging at a pinafore she wore over her clothes.

"This is Mrs Jenkins," said PC Ian Richards to Sgt Ross. "Her husband, Stan, went out to the local shop first thing this morning but hasn't come back.

"His memory isn't so good these days and he may have forgotten how to get home.

"I've checked with the shop and Mr Jenkins didn't get there to do his little bit of shopping. He could be anywhere," PC Richards added.

Mrs Jenkins came forward to Sgt Ross. "I'm so worried officer," she told him.

"Stan has been getting worse with his memory and I've no idea what could have happened to him. I just hope he's all right." Sgt Ross did his best to calm Mrs Jenkins down. "I'm sure we'll find him," he said.

"He can't have got far and Boo here is brilliant at tracking. Do you have a piece of Stan's clothes that she can sniff and get his scent?" he asked.

Mrs Jenkins went back into the bungalow and returned a minute later with a dark red shirt. "Stan was wearing this one yesterday and it hasn't been washed yet. Will this do?" she asked the police officer.

Sgt Ross said it would be perfect and he put it under Boo's nose so she could have a good sniff.

The policeman was always amazed at the dogs' sense of smell, which was up to 100,000 times more powerful than a human's, and after a few seconds Boo put her nose to the ground and started tugging on her lead.

"She's picked up a good scent already Mrs Jenkins," said Sgt Ross. "If any dog can find your husband, Boo can. She's marvel..."

He didn't finish his sentence or hear the reply from Mrs Jenkins because Boo was already tugging hard on her lead and following the scent.

They disappeared around the corner while he was still speaking and PC Richards was left to explain to Mrs Jenkins what was going on.

"Boo has picked up a strong scent already and she will lead the sergeant to Mr Jenkins. We'll soon have your husband back," he told her in a reassuring voice.

"Oh, I do hope so," said Mrs Jenkins. "We've been married for 60 years and have hardly spent a day apart.

"I just want my Stan back, safe and well." She gave a little sob and dabbed her damp eyes with a handkerchief.

PC Richards put an arm on her shoulder and told her: "I'm sure it will be alright now we've got Boo on the case," he said.

Around the corner from them, Boo was moving fast and sniffing the ground where Mr Jenkins had walked earlier that morning.

Out of Myrtle Crescent they went and on to the main road that led to the local shop but before they reached the shop, Boo tugged at her lead to tell Sgt Ross to turn left.

They were now heading towards some woods and Boo kept going fast, past Robinson's Garage and past Elsie's Café, with Boo still picking up a strong scent.

A minute later they were at the edge of the woods and Boo led Sgt Ross down a muddy track into the wilderness.

On they went, past some picnic tables and towards a small pond where three ducks were gently swimming along the surface.

Boo led Sgt Ross around the edge of the pond and the policeman began to get concerned, hoping the old man hadn't lost his footing and ended up in the water.

But seconds later, Boo was off again, this time

heading away from the pond and deeper into the centre of the woods.

Sgt Ross breathed a sigh of relief that Mr Jenkins had walked away from the pond and soon they were heading up a gentle slope, with trees and bushes all around.

The track became even more muddy and Sgt Ross was finding it hard to stop himself from slipping as Boo carried on further into the woods.

She still had a strong scent and was excitedly following it. Sgt Ross wondered to himself if Mr Jenkins could have walked very much further and just as he was thinking that, Boo stopped and barked, a signal that she was very close to the source of the scent.

Sgt Ross told Boo "Good girl," and looked around him but couldn't see anyone. He called out "Mr Jenkins. Can you hear me?" and then listened hard for a reply.

At first all he could hear was the wind whistling through the trees but just a few seconds later he heard a faint "hello, hello. I'm here."

It was coming from the right hand side of the path and Sgt Ross saw crushed weeds as if someone had walked that way.

He followed the trail and as he turned a corner he saw an old man sitting on a tree stump.

"Can you help me? My legs are tangled up in brambles," the old man said.

"Are you Mr Jenkins?" Sgt Ross asked.

"Mr who?" the old man replied. "I can't remember my name."

It must be Mr Jenkins, Sgt Ross thought. He had been given a description of what he'd been wearing and this old man matched that exactly.

"What are you doing here?" the policeman asked.

"I'm going to the shop. We need some bread," Mr Jenkins replied.

Sgt Ross went with Boo to where Mr Jenkins was sitting and used a pen knife to cut the brambles which were wrapped around his legs.

Once the old man's legs were free, Sgt Ross told him to lean on his shoulder for support and he began to lead him back to the path.

"Where are we going? Is the shop here?" Mr Jenkins asked in a confused state.

"We're going to take you home first. We can get some bread later," Sgt Ross told him as Boo led the way back to the path.

Once there, he sat Mr Jenkins down on another tree stump and told him he was going to make a call.

He used his radio to report to the control room that Mr Jenkins had been found and told the controller to get a message to the old man's worried wife.

Afterwards he checked that Mr Jenkins was all right to carry on walking out of the woods and Mr Jenkins told him: "Of course I am, I'm in the army, fit as a fiddle!" and he set off down the path.

He clearly was in good physical shape and in his mind was a young soldier back in his army days, not a confused old man.

He walked without needing any help and a few minutes later Boo led them out of the woods towards the main road, past the café and the garage.

Boo trotted along beside Sgt Ross and Mr Jenkins and as the little group entered Myrtle Crescent, relieved Mrs Jenkins came running towards them.

"Oh Stan, thank heavens you're all right," she said. "Of course I am," said Mr Jenkins. "I've only been to the shop."

Mrs Jenkins raised her eyebrows towards Sgt Ross and took her husband indoors.

She then returned to tell Sgt Ross "thank you so much for finding Stan. He's getting more and more confused and I'm going to have to get some help looking after him."

Sgt Ross told her it was Boo who deserved the thanks and she leant down and scratched Boo behind the ears.

"Thank you Boo. I don't know what we would have done without you."

Sgt Ross proudly agreed. "She's one of the best dogs I've ever had. Brilliant at everything," he told Mrs Jenkins.

"We'd better get back to the station. Someone else might be needing Boo's help."

Sgt Ross put Boo into the back of his van and

waved to PC Richards as he set off to return to the station.

He was satisfied with the morning's work and now had to wait for the next job.

PC Richards was left to make sure everything was all right and he waited for the doctor to come and give Stan a check over.

Physically, Mr Jenkins was in good order but the doctor said he would get in contact with social services to see what help they could give in looking after him.

A few minutes later Sgt Ross and Boo returned to the station.

Another busy week lay ahead for them and the rest of the Tingleside dog unit!

"Boo is one of the best dogs I've ever had. Brilliant at everything,"

Getting on The Road

Earlier that morning, Chloe Marsden had taken about 20 minutes to walk to the park where the circus was packed up and ready to go.

As she arrived everything was quiet and it was clear the lorries wouldn't be moving off until dawn, which was still over two hours away.

Chloe ducked under a rope which separated the vehicles from the rest of the park and started to walk around the lorries and caravans.

She wanted to avoid the caravans, where people were still asleep, and instead concentrated on the lorries, some of which had heavy canvass covers tied down with ropes.

Chloe tugged at one of the ropes but it was tied so tightly that there was no movement.

She tried another, and then another but they were all too tight. She began to wonder if she would ever find one that was a bit loose.

Then she tugged at one which allowed a little more movement.

Excitedly she pulled at the rope and to her delight it slowly but surely became more relaxed in her fingers.

Soon it was loose enough so that Chloe was able to pull the canvas cover open a little.

Looking around to make sure no-one was watching, she wriggled underneath the canvas.

It was dark and quiet and using the torch on her mobile phone, Chloe could make out steps up to a platform.

Up ahead was a section of seating for the big top. "Perfect," Chloe thought and she pulled herself up to the platform and then on to the section of bench seating above.

She put her rucksack on to the bench and used that as a pillow as she settled down and waited.

The clock on her phone said it was 4.29 am and she switched off the torch feature and lay quietly in the dark.

She didn't want to go back to sleep so stayed alert to listen for any activity, worried in case she was discovered...

"What if someone finds me here," she thought but as the minutes ticked by she became more relaxed in her hiding place.

Then, soon after 6 am, she began to hear voices as the circus staff started to wake up and prepare to set off.

Someone was walking around the outside of the lorries, checking that everything was tied down securely enough.

As Chloe had found a few hours earlier, most of the ropes were good and tight.

Then Chloe became nervous as the man came to the place where she had loosened the rope to get in.

Chloe held her breath and didn't make a sound as the loose rope was examined. Then, to her relief, she heard him call out,

"Hey, Andy, did you tie this one down?"

Then the reply, "No, it was that new lad, Tony. He'll need to learn to make them tighter. I've had to re-do one of his on the other side."

The first man complained about "sending a boy to do a man's job" then rather than examine the rope any further, Chloe just heard the rope being pulled tighter.

"That's done it," the man shouted out to Andy. "It's tight enough now."

Chloe had escaped being found and silently she thanked Tony for not doing a thorough job tying the rope.

"There's no way I'd get in here now," she thought to herself as she prepared for the next stage in her adventure.

She heard the two men moving on to the next section of lorries to check on the ropes, completely unaware that a stowaway had sneaked in and was hiding on one of the benches!

Half an hour later Chloe heard the first lorry start its engine, followed seconds later by another and then another until they were all were ready to set off.

She was glad of a section of ironwork railings which she was able to wrap an arm around to keep herself secure as the lorry moved off.

They had started the drive to the next town where the circus would be setting up.

Chloe didn't know where it would be, all she knew was that she was on her way to realizing her plan of joining the circus. As the lorries hit the open road and began to speed up she felt excited and nervous in equal parts.

An hour later and with the lorries still on the road, there was activity at Merrymeet Children's Care Home.

It would soon be breakfast time and the staff were going from room to room making sure all the children were awake and getting ready for school.

Miss Hargreaves knocked on Chloe's door and announced it was time to get up.

When she heard no reply she shouted out "I'm coming in sleepyhead. Wakey wakey!"

She opened the door ready to give Chloe a shake to get her moving.

The curtains were still shut tight but there was just enough light for Miss Hargreaves to make out the shape of what she assumed was a dozing girl under the covers.

"Come on, time to get moving," she said as she opened the curtains, letting the light flood in.

But when there was no reply she turned around and stood beside the bed.

It's not like Chloe to not get up when told to, Miss Hargreaves thought to herself, preparing to give her a shake.

"Come on lazybones," she said as she pulled the covers back.

She expected to find a sleepyhead Chloe. But instead all she found was two pillows made to look like the shape of someone asleep!

"Oh no," she cried out, confused about what could have happened.

She ran out of the door and down the corridor to the office of Mrs Jessop, the manageress.

She knocked and then opened the door without waiting for a reply and called out in a panic: "Chloe's missing. She's not in her room."

Mrs Jessop quickly came out of her office and followed Miss Hargreaves back to Chloe's room to see for herself.

"She must have run away," Miss Hargreaves said and Mrs Jessop told her to start searching the rest of the house while she called the police.

Miss Hargreaves went from room to room looking for Chloe, with the panic increasing with every failed search.

Twenty minutes later every room had been searched without any sign of Chloe.

No-one had any idea what had happened and the front doorbell rang as the police arrived.

No-one knew that by now Chloe was miles away and with the circus as it moved on towards its next town.

Chloe had been lying still and quiet for about three hours before she felt the lorry slow down as it came off the motorway and towards the next town.

They had been in a big park in a town in Berkshire before and were now further west, arriving at the town of Leymouth where they were due to set up in a park beside the sea.

As the lorries pulled to a stop Chloe lay as still as could be and heard voices from people getting down from their cabs.

"This looks a nice spot," Chloe heard someone say.

But she couldn't see anything from her hiding place and she stayed still and quiet as the noise of activity increased around her.

She could hear ropes being untied and the light started to increase as canvases around her were removed.

She sat frozen in her hiding place as she heard the rope holding her canvas being untied. "Am I about to be discovered?" she thought to herself.

But then to her relief Chloe heard someone say: "Come on lads, let' s go and find a cafe before the caravans arrive."

She lay still as she heard others agreeing that finding breakfast was the most important thing.

She bent down to get out from underneath the canvas and for the first time she saw where she was, with a beach and then the sea beyond

She had got away with it so far and as she heard the men leaving, the canvas covering her hiding place was left untied and flapping loose.

Gently she sat up and then slithered downwards until her feet hit the ground.

She bent down to get out from underneath the canvas and for the first time she saw where she was, with a beach and then the sea beyond the park where they had settled.

Putting her rucksack back over her shoulder, she squeezed between the lorries into the space where the big top was obviously going to be put up.

She sat on a rock and took out a packet of shortbread fingers which she had in her rucksack and ate the lot as she waited for the next bout of activity.

She had managed the first part of her plan to run away to the circus, now she had to make sure she wouldn't be sent straight back to the children's home!

Finding Chloe

Back in Tingleside, Bruin was enjoying his lie-in, as he watched Mrs Wilkie busying herself in the kitchen.

She had two birthday cakes to make and all the ingredients were set out in front of her as she finished working out the designs for both cakes.

The rocket shaped cake was easy but the horse and rider one was more complicated, particularly as the horse had to be jumping over some poles.

But she had managed to work out a design and the next stage was baking the sponges which would then need to be carefully cut into the correct shapes.

Once that was done Mrs Wilkie would be making different coloured icings to cover the shaped sponges and their buttercream fillings.

But that would all be done tomorrow. Now she just had to wait for the sponges to finish baking.

Then it would be time to take Bruin out for a

HAPPY
BiRTHD

The rocket shaped cake was easy but the horse and rider one was more complicated, particularly as the horse had to be jumping over some poles.

walk while the sponges cooled down before they were ready to be cut into shape.

At Merrymeet Children's Home Mrs Jessop, the manageress, was in her office with Miss Hargreaves, the care worker who had discovered Chloe was missing, and two police officers.

"This is a photograph of Chloe," Mrs Jessop was saying as she handed over a picture of Chloe standing in the garden.

"When was it taken?" asked PC Harry Trimble.

Mrs Jessop looked at Miss Hargreaves, who would know better about dates.

"Two months ago," said Miss Hargreaves and both police officers nodded to show they were pleased that the photograph was so recent.

"We take new photographs of all the children every six months so that we always have up to date pictures in case something like this happens," Mrs Jessop said.

"I can't believe Chloe has gone missing, she's such a sensible child and she's normally so well behaved."

PC Trimble explained that they would need to speak to Chloe's best friends in case any of them had an idea about where she might have gone.

"That would be Megan and Tilly," said Miss Hargreaves. "I'll go and fetch them."

She left the room to find both girls, who had been kept from going to school in case they were needed by the police.

Two minutes later she was back in the office with Megan and Tilly and explained to the girls that the police officers wanted to speak to them about Chloe.

"We don't know anything. She never told us she was going to run away," said Tilly but PC Trimble explained that they needed to interview both girls.

"You might know more actually than you realise," he told them.

His colleague, PC Emma Rawlings, invited both girls to sit down and smiled at them to put them at their ease before beginning her questions.

"When did you last see Chloe?" she asked and both girls said it was last night, as they all watched television in the home's sitting room.

"Did she give you any idea she was planning to run away?" and both girls shook their heads.

"We were shocked when we heard. She seemed perfectly normal last night," said Megan.

The two police officers asked more questions, with the girls both saying again and again that they did not know of Chloe's plans and had no idea where she might have gone.

But then Miss Hargreaves said: "Didn't you all go to the circus on Saturday night?"

PC Rawlings showed special interest in that.

There were stories of children running away to join the circus but she didn't think it really happened these days.

Even so, it was worth following up the fact that they had been to the circus.

"What did Chloe think of the circus? Did she say anything about it afterwards?" she asked.

Both girls bit their bottom lips and looked at each other.

"They obviously know something," PC Rawlings thought to herself and Mrs Jessop spoke next.

"If you know something you must tell the police. It's not being disloyal to Chloe.

"She could be in danger and we need to do all we can to make sure she is safe," she said gently.

Both girls looked at each other again. "We'd better say,"

Megan whispered to Tilly, who nodded her head in agreement.

Megan turned to the police officers. "She might have said something," she said.

PC Rawlings leaned forward and looked kindly from one girl to the other. "What did she say?" she asked quietly.

"Only that it would be fun to join the circus. We didn't think she was serious," said Tilly, almost in a whisper.

"Do you think that's where she's gone?" asked PC Trimble.

"We don't know. She didn't say she was going to run away.

"We thought she'd forget all about it once we got back here," said Tilly.

PC Trimble turned to Mrs Jessop to ask where the circus had been.

"It was in the park in the middle of town but I think they were moving on today.

"I don't know where they were going next," Mrs Jessop said and the two police officers looked at each other.

"It sounds like that's where she might have gone," said PC Trimble to his colleague as they prepared to leave the room.

"You won't tell her we told you. She'd never trust us again," Megan said.

PC Rawlings assured her: "We won't say anything but you've done the right thing telling us. It's very important we find Chloe as soon as possible and make sure she is all right.

"She's only 13 and she needs to be somewhere safe," she said before following PC Trimble through the door to pass on the news to the control room.

Once outside the office, PC Rawlings turned to her colleague. "That must be where she's gone. Control will have to find out where the circus has moved on to and we must hope we can find Chloe," she said.

In her heart she really hoped the young teenager would be safe and sound and found very quickly.

As a girl, Emma Rawlings had herself had dreams of seeing the world but she never did anything about it and now, as a grown-up, she was glad she had finished school and settled down into a really useful job with the police.

She had joined the force because she wanted to help people and now, helping Chloe and making sure she was safe and sound, was the most important thing.

She knew from reading Chloe's case file at the children's home that she had gone there at the age of just nine after both her parents died in a car crash.

She had no brothers or sisters or other family but had been given a home at Merrymeet and had settled in well.

Emma felt sad about Chloe losing her parents and it brought back memories of her own sister, Susan, who had been very ill from birth and died at the age of just seven.

As a toddler Susan had been a bundle of fun and never let her illness stop her enjoying herself.

It was only in her last months that Susan had mostly been confined to her bed.

The tragedy of when she died had deeply affected all of Emma's family and was a big part of what had made her want to help others and by the age of 12 she knew she wanted to join the police.

Now, aged 23, every night when she went home to her cat, Jasper, she felt satisfaction at the work she had done.

But a little piece of her heart still missed her sister Susan, and that drove her on to do her best for others.

Having a missing girl, who was a teenager as Susan would have now been, brought back all her memories and made her determined to do her best to find her.

"Don't worry Chloe, we'll make sure you're safe and well," she said to herself as she and PC Trimble left the children's home and prepared to return to their station.

Once back at the station the two officers made a report about Chloe and spoke to their sergeant to tell him of their suspicions that Chloe had run off to the circus.

“Well, the first thing is to find out where the circus was going,” said Sgt Grant Tucker and both PCs agreed and went back to their desks.

Emma fired up her computer and typed the name of the circus into the search engine.

Within a second the website of Mr Pickering’s Amazing Circus had sprung up and there, on the left hand side, was a heading “Our next shows.”

She clicked on the link and up came the information that the circus would be appearing in Leymouth every night that week from Tuesday until Saturday.

After that it would be heading down the coast to a place called Tingleside to appear the following week.

“I’ve got the information,” Emma called out to PC Trimble and told him about the next two venues for the circus.

“Leymouth and Tingleside are both out of our patch. We’ll have to pass it on to the local force,” said PC Trimble and he picked up the telephone to call Leymouth police.

It was only a small station and was answered on about the 20th ring, with an out of breath voice saying “Leymouth Police, how can I help?”

The out of breath voice belonged to PC Tom Dyson who was already exhausted by his growing workload.

He explained that he was the only officer on duty all that week and he already had two burglaries to deal with, as well as a farmer who had dumped a load of manure outside his bank as a protest.

But he promised to check at the circus for the missing girl and PC Trimble passed the news on to Emma.

"Hmmm," she thought to herself. "It doesn't sound very encouraging," and a thought started to come into her head.

She had a week off from the following Monday and if there was still no news of Chloe she might spend the holiday in Tingleside, which just happened to be where the circus was going next!

She stood back to admire the shiny red and silver coloured machine and felt very pleased with her purchase.

Bruin had finally stirred, sitting up to see what was going on.

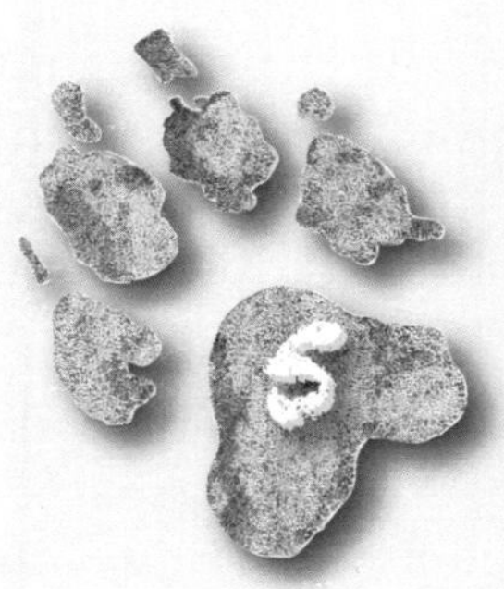

Adventure on The Beach

Bruin had been happy to stay in his bed as Mrs Wilkie did her work but now it was after lunchtime and he was ready for his walk.

But just as his lead was about to be attached and he was taken out the telephone rang and Mrs Wilkie put the lead back on its hook and then went to answer the phone.

"Oh, hello Brenda," Mrs Wilkie said, hearing that it was her friend Brenda Blewitt who lived down the road.

Brenda was a good friend but one of life's worriers and Mrs Wilkie listened as Brenda began to speak about her latest troubles.

"Why don't you come round and we'll put the kettle on and you can tell me all about it," Bruin heard Mrs Wilkie say.

"That doesn't sound good. What about our walk?" Bruin thought as Mrs Wilkie came back into the kitchen and filled the kettle with water.

"Sorry Bruin, change of plan," she said over her shoulder as she put the kettle on. "Our walk will have to wait, Brenda needs to come round for a cuppa and a chat."

Bruin put his head down and trooped back to his bed. "Well, there are worse places to be," he thought as he snuggled down again and a couple of minutes later there was a knock at the kitchen door and then Brenda let herself in.

"Here we are Brenda," Mrs Wilkie said. "Tea and biscuits and a good chat and soon everything will seem a lot better."

Bruin didn't bother wagging his tail or lifting his head as Brenda came in and he was relieved when the two women took their tea and biscuits into the sitting room.

"Do you want to come too?" Mrs Wilkie asked Bruin but he made it clear he was happier staying in his bed.

The last thing he wanted was to join them and have to listen to Brenda's latest problems!

He knew the children would be home a bit later and perhaps they'd go out then.

It must have been two hours before Brenda left.

As she walked out of the kitchen door she was telling Mrs Wilkie "I feel so much better now. Thanks for listening to my worries."

Bruin perked up again, thinking perhaps it was walk time now and and cheered up even more when just a few minutes later the kitchen door opened again. In came Henry and Harriet after walking home from school.

They both called out "hello Bruin" as they entered the kitchen and Bruin got out of his bed with his tail wagging.

Ten minutes later Florence arrived home and gave Bruin a friendly stroke before saying hello to the others from the family.

"Has Bruin been out?" she asked and when told there hadn't been a chance because Brenda had come around Florence suggested they all go out for a walk.

"That's more like it," thought Bruin and within five minutes Mrs Wilkie had made a flask of tea and she and the children were ready to go out and were putting Bruin's lead back on.

"Can I call Jasmine and see if she wants to come?" asked Florence and a quick telephone call later and it was arranged to meet Jasmine on the beach.

They decided that while on the beach they would pick up plastic litter to stop it being washed back out to sea.

Henry fetched a big canvas bag from the cupboard and the little party set off for the beach, with Bruin happily tugging at his lead to encourage them to go faster.

It was a grey, cloudy and windy afternoon and Jasmine was waiting at the entrance to the beach for when they arrived.

Jasmine's mother had been Bruin's official

"puppy walker" before he began his police training and Jasmine and her friends all loved Bruin very much.

Now he was with his new family but Jasmine was invited to join them on walks regularly, which she was very pleased about!

There were only a few other dog walkers on the beach and once they reached the sand, Bruin's lead was unclipped and he charged away, with Henry chasing him.

"Oh, this is lovely," said Mrs Wilkie as she felt the salty sea air on her face.

She had hold of the canvas bag and Florence had brought a litter picker, which had a sort of claw at the end which could be used to pick things up.

Straight away Florence, Harriet and Jasmine started to pick up plastic bottles, crisp packets and other bits of rubbish.

Some of it was dropped by untidy people who didn't seem to care about the damage they were causing and some was washed in from the sea.

The family had watched a nature programme about the amount of plastic in the sea which showed that fish, turtles, seals and other animals were mistaking the plastic for food and swallowing it.

Some birds and fish that had died and been washed ashore had been found to have balls of plastic blocking their insides, the programme had said.

Bruin had made friends with Tommy, who was a spotty Dalmatian, and when the pair saw each other they started a friendly game of chase, both tearing across the beach as fast as they possibly could.

From that day on the family had become determined to play their tiny part in reducing the amount of plastic in the oceans so always took their rubbish bag with them when they went to the beach.

Bruin and Henry were by now running close to the water's edge where the sand was still damp and much firmer.

Bruin had made friends with Tommy, who was a spotty Dalmatian, and when the pair saw each other they started a friendly game of chase, both tearing across the beach as fast as they possibly could.

Henry became puffed out running after them and by the time the others had walked down to join him he was bending over with his hands on his knees and breathing hard.

"Where's Bruin?" asked Mrs Wilkie and Henry told her: "Tommy was down here and they ran off together. I don't know where they are now."

Just then Tommy's owner, Mrs Westaway, came into view, with Tommy trotting beside her.

"Have you seen Bruin? He was with Tommy," asked Mrs Wilkie.

"I'm afraid not," said Mrs Westaway. "Tommy came back about five minutes ago but there was no sign of Bruin."

"Oh dear, where can Bruin have gone? It's not like him to go missing like this," said Mrs Wilkie and all the family began to get concerned.

The tide was coming in and soon the area where

they were standing would be covered with salty seawater.

"Let's look over here," suggested Florence, aiming for rocks at the back of the beach and the family and Jasmine headed there, all shouting "Bruin, Bruin, where are you?"

But there was no sign of the dog, no matter how loud they shouted.

They headed along the beach to where Salvatore's Café was based, serving tea, coffee, cakes and sandwiches to beach goers.

Mr Salvatore, who was known by all his customers as Sal, was just closing for the day and was outside taking in his signs advertising the day's menu.

He knew all the local dogs and kept an old sweets jar filled with dog treats to hand out to them and it was just the sort of place Bruin may have headed for.

But as Mrs Wilke went ahead to ask Sal if he had seen Bruin the children could see him shaking his head.

Mrs Wilkie walked back to them looking even more worried, telling the children Bruin hadn't been seen at the cafe.

Henry started to blame himself for Bruin going missing and tears filled his eyes but Mrs Wilkie bent down to him, making sure he knew it wasn't his fault.

Florence, Harriet and Jasmine all said the same thing to the younger boy.

But Henry was still feeling guilty and as the afternoon light began to fade with still no sign of Bruin, Henry couldn't stop his tears rolling down his cheeks.

The group continued to search for Bruin, asking everyone they came to if they had seen him but no-one had.

As the clock ticked around to 5pm and getting closer to tea time they were all getting really concerned and worried.

"We'll have to go home soon," said Mrs Wilkie. "It will be getting dark but I'm sure Bruin will be able to find his way back home."

"Maybe he's already gone home," said worried Florence hopefully.

Mrs Wilkie said "let's check" and pulled out her mobile phone to call their next door neighbours, Mr and Mrs Hedges.

She asked if they could look outside and see if Bruin was standing by the front door, waiting to be let in.

The children waited anxiously for an answer but when they heard their mother say, "oh well, it was worth a try. Thank you for looking," they knew Bruin hadn't been spotted standing outside the door.

The little group were by now getting tired, cold and hungry but they walked the entire length of the beach to call for Bruin.

They reached the rocks at the left hand end as the tide was getting higher and covering some of the rocks.

There was still no answer so they started to walk back towards other end of the beach, starting to get really worried.

They were all shouting and looking as hard as they could in the fading light and getting more and more concerned.

Suddenly though there was a familiar sound. They all stopped to listen as they heard the unmistakable noise of Bruin's bark!

It was coming from up ahead, at the other end of the beach.

It definitely was Bruin's bark and suddenly they all spotted the much loved pet running across the sand towards them.

"It's Bruin!" Henry shouted as he ran towards the tan and black German Shepherd.

But before Henry and the others reached Bruin, the dog stood on his back legs, barking loudly.

He spun around to face the direction he had come from and barked some more, clearly getting agitated.

"What's wrong Bruin?" Florence asked as the family reached him.

But Bruin just barked some more and then started to run back towards the rocks right at the other end of the beach.

"He wants us to follow him," said Harriet and the children and Mrs Wilkie set off to run after Bruin.

A few minutes later they reached the other end

of the beach and saw Bruin scampering over the rocks.

They shouted to him to come back but he took no notice.

The tide was by now lapping around their feet and they were jolly glad they were all in Wellington boots.

They knew that it would only be a few minutes before the water would come right over the top of their boots if they stayed where they were.

They saw Bruin climbing up the rocks until he reached what looked like the edge of a drop and he stopped, turned towards the family and started to bark again.

"What is it Bruin? What's wrong?" Florence called out to him.

She wanted to follow him but her mother said it was too dangerous in the fading light to climb over the dark and slippery rocks.

"Be quiet everyone," Harriet suddenly said. "I think I can hear something."

The family and Jasmine all strained their ears and Bruin stopped barking, leaving just the sound of the waves and the seagulls.

"Did you hear that?" asked Harriet, who had clearly heard something else.

"I did," said Jasmine. "It was someone shouting."

They all listened even harder until they could all hear the unmistakable sound of a voice calling out "Help, help. Is anyone there?"

Mrs Wilkie was the first to answer. "We can hear you. Where are you?"

"I'm on the rocks," came the voice. "I'm cut off by the tide and the water is up to my knees."

"We're going to get help for you," shouted Jasmine.

"What's your name?" she shouted and the boy answered "It's Joe. Please help me, the tide is getting higher all the time."

By now Mrs Wilkie was on her telephone, calling the coastguard to report that someone was cut off by the tide at Tingleside beach.

"We're sending the inshore lifeboat. They'll be there in a few minutes. Make sure you keep yourselves safe and away from the water," said the coastguard.

By now the water was half way up Mrs Wilkie's boots and she told the children to all walk back up the beach to dry sand.

"But what about Bruin?" asked Harriet and they could see that his route back to the beach was now covered in water, making it dangerous for him to get back.

"I don't know," said Mrs Wilkie in a worried voice and just then they spotted the inshore lifeboat as it shone a bright spotlight on to the rocks to locate the cut off person.

The boat came close to the rocks and the lifeboat crew spotted the teenage boy, standing in water which was now almost up to his waist.

"Can you walk to us?" asked one of the lifeboat

crew and Joe shouted back "I think so," and started to wade out towards the boat.

But as he walked he slipped on some rocks covered in slimy seaweed and his head went under the water.

The lifeboat crew knew it was a really dangerous situation but the boat couldn't get to him because there were too many sharp rocks.

They watched in horror as the boy splashed about in the water and they shouted to him to try to swim towards their boat.

But it was clear that as hard as the boy tried, the waves kept pushing him back towards the jagged rocks.

There was clearly a real danger that he could be thrown against the sharp rocks by a wave and he was clearly struggling to keep his head above the water.

"I'm going in after him," bravely shouted one of the lifeboat crew, willing to risk his own life to save the boy.

Suddenly though the crew were amazed to see a black and tan German Shepherd dog leap off the rocks into the water and swim towards the boy.

The dog got right beside the boy and the lad reached out his hand towards him.

He wrapped one arm around the dog's neck and hung on as tight as he could as the brave animal swam towards the boat.

The waves were getting bigger as the dog and boy fought their way towards the boat, with the lifeboat crew all shouting encouragement.

It was really hard work but the dog kept going with the boy hanging on to him.

Finally they were close enough for two of the lifeboat crew to reach down and pull the soaking wet teenager out of the water.

He was wrapped in a foil blanket to warm him up but he wasn't thinking about himself, but about Bruin, who was still being thrown about in the rough sea.

"Quick, you've got to get the dog. He saved my life. I think his name is Bruin," the exhausted boy panted.

"Oh I know Bruin," said the person in charge of the lifeboat, who was also the local butcher, and he started calling to Bruin to come to them.

Bruin was swimming hard just to stop himself being swept onto the sharp rocks but he was clearly getting exhausted.

For a second the lifeboat crew thought they could reach him but then another huge wave carried Bruin back towards the rocks and away from the boat.

"Come on Bruin," shouted Joe and all the lifeboat crew as they watched him fighting against the waves.

With one last massive effort Bruin managed to get alongside the lifeboat and the two men who had pulled the boy on board then reached down and managed to grab hold of him.

They pulled with all their strength to get Bruin

out of the water and into the boat, where Joe threw his arms around the dog and then wrapped his foil blanket around him.

Back on the beach the family heard Joe shouting, "I'm in the boat now and Bruin is with me!"

"Did you hear that?" asked Harriet as Joe shouted from the boat.

The others said they did and there was great relief that the lad and Bruin were now both safe.

Back on board the lifeboat one of the crew told Joe: "You had a lucky escape there.

"The tide is coming in really fast and within a few minutes you'd have been out of your depth."

"I can't believe I'm safe. And it's thanks to you and to Bruin that I've made it," Joe replied.

"I'm glad we were able to get here quickly," said the lifeboat leader.

"But it's Bruin who was the real hero. I'll make sure there's a sausage for him the next time he is taken for a walk past my butcher's shop!"

The lifeboat continued to be rocked by heavy waves as it headed around to the beach.

Finally it made it and Joe and Bruin were put safely on to the sand and Joe thanked the crew for all they had done.

"That's what we're here for," said one of the men as the boat motored away from the beach and back towards its base.

Joe and Bruin were greeted by Mrs Wilkie and the children and Joe explained that he was 13 years old and on his first fishing trip on to the rocks without his dad.

"He is always telling me to be careful about being cut off by the tide.

"He'll be mad with me when he hears I got stuck. Without you all and Bruin I don't know what would have happened.

"The water was getting deeper and deeper and would soon have been over my head," said Joe.

"Bruin really has saved my life.

"He found me as the water was starting to come in and stayed with me until it was getting really dangerous," he explained.

"Bruin tried to show me the best way to escape over the rocks but it was too slippery and dangerous. All I could do was stand back and watch him scamper away.

"He looked back at me just before he went out of sight as if to say 'you'll be alright, I'm going to get help' and then he was gone," Joe said.

"That must have been when he came and told us to follow him," said Florence.

"Yes, it was just a few minutes later that I saw him again and then heard all of you shouting," said Joe.

"I couldn't believe it. Bruin led you to me and I knew then that the alarm would be raised."

Joe then told the story of him slipping in the water and Bruin swimming out to him and helping him towards the lifeboat.

They watched in horror as the boy splashed about in the water and they shouted to him to try to swim towards their boat.
RNLI

RNLI

"He saved my life. He certainly is a very special dog," said Joe.

That was something everyone could agree with!

Joe was given a cup of hot tea from Mrs Wilkie's flask and the children gathered around Bruin and wrapped their arms around him, telling him what a clever boy he was.

By now a small crowd had gathered on the beach to watch the drama and they all clapped as Joe and the others – and Bruin – walked up the beach to the road.

"Will you be alright to get home?" Mrs Wilkie asked Joe and he said he lived less than a hundred yards away.

"Well, we'll leave you to get home and explain why you're so wet!" Mrs Wilkie said and so Joe, after giving Bruin one last cuddle walked back to his house.

"What a day!" said Jasmine as she prepared to walk back to her house. "It seems there's always some excitement when Bruin is around!"

The others agreed it had been quite a trip to the beach and as Jasmine set off to walk home, the family and Bruin headed back to their house.

They arrived back into the warm and peaceful kitchen. It was time for some well-earned toast and strawberry jam and some extra special biscuits for Bruin!

Chloe's First Day With The Circus

Chloe had made sure she kept out of sight as the men returned from the café and started to put the circus big top together.

An hour later the caravans arrived bringing the circus performers and other workers and the area became noisy and lively as preparations started to be made.

All day long the circus slowly began to take shape and by the early evening the big top was up and ready.

The seats were all in place and the caravans were filled with the smells of meals being cooked and the noise of people chattering and laughing.

Inside the big top the acts started to practice.

First it was the acrobats, who called themselves Los Tumberleros.

They raced from one side of the circus ring to the other as they put in a series of cartwheels, tumbles and backward and forward flips.

Chloe had sneaked into the big top and looked on in wonder as the acrobats went through their incredible routines.

Then someone shouted "we have to practice the pyramid" and five of the acrobats stood in a line as three others spun forwards and bounced up on to their shoulders.

Then two more jumped as if their feet had springs and they landed on the shoulders of the row of three.

Finally one acrobat ran forward, did an incredible cartwheel and jumped forward to land right at the top.

He then did a juggling act before doing a forwards flip to land back on the ground and Chloe had to stop herself from bursting into a round of applause.

She sat on her hands to keep them still, knowing that any sound would give her away.

Next, one of the acrobats produced a piece of equipment with five large rings, one on top of the other. One of the other acrobats did a forward roll through the bottom ring.

Then another did the same through the second ring and so on until an acrobat flipped through the highest ring and Chloe again had to stop herself from bursting into applause.

The next people to practice were the trapeze artists, sisters Lucinda and Evelyn Fox and who called themselves the Flying Foxes.

It was seeing them on Saturday night that had

Chloe had sneaked into the big top and looked on in wonder as the acrobats went through their incredible routines.

really excited Chloe and made her want to join the circus.

"If only I could do that one day," she thought to herself as the Flying Foxes began their routine, swinging on their bars and then one flying through the air, spinning three times and being caught by the other.

As she watched the incredible performance she was unaware of a person walking up behind her but suddenly a gruff voice disturbed her concentration. "What are you doing here?" the man asked.

Chloe didn't know what to say but then the man asked "haven't you got any work to do?" Chloe thought quickly and answered, "Er, no. We've finished what we were doing."

She just hoped he wouldn't ask what she had actually been doing because she wouldn't know what to say.

"Well, you'd better take this box of tickets and put them in the kiosk. We'll be starting to sell them tomorrow," the man said and he handed a cardboard box to Chloe.

"OK, will do," Chloe said and she carried the box out of the big top.

She blinked as the sunlight from outside of the big top dazzled her eyes but as she got used to it, she saw people everywhere busily preparing for the show.

As she walked around to the other side, where the sales kiosk was, she realised that if she looked like she was doing something useful people would just assume she was part of the team and would not ask her awkward questions.

So she marched as if she really belonged there and soon reached the sales kiosk.

When she got there she opened the door and prepared to leave the box but to her surprise someone was in there.

"Ah, those must be the tickets," the young woman in the kiosk said.

"Yes," said Chloe. "Ready to be sold from tomorrow morning."

"Excellent. Just leave them there," the woman said, pointing to a spot on the floor.

Chloe put the box down and turned to leave but the woman said: "Are you new here? I don't think I've seen you before."

Again Chloe had to think on her feet. "Yes, we've just joined."

"Oh, OK," said the woman. "Are you here with your parents?"

Again had Chloe had to think quickly. "Er, yes. My dad is one of the set builders," she said.

So now not only was she pretending she belonged there, she had made up a whole family. This could be getting awkward, she thought.

But the woman just said: "Well, I hope you all like it. It's a tough life but a good one if you don't mind hard work. I'll see you round."

And then she turned back to what she had been

doing and Chloe was able to leave the kiosk.

She had managed to avoid being found out so far but it was now evening time and all she'd had to eat all day was the pack of shortbread fingers she'd brought with her.

Also, she had no idea where she was going to sleep that night and the reality of her situation began to hit home.

Her warm and comfortable bed at the children's home seemed a million miles away and she started to wonder what Megan, Tilly and the others had had for tea and what they were up to.

She walked back to the other side of the big top and to her relief the practice session was over and everything was quiet.

She walked up to the seats and sat down.

It was dark and chilly and she was feeling hungry. Had she done the right thing? she wondered but it was too soon to give up on her plan.

And as she settled down she started to daydream about joining the Flying Foxes on their trapeze wires, forgetting how hungry she was and how uncomfortable her night ahead was likely to be.

Despite everything, she managed to get to sleep and her dreams were filled with the excitement of life in the circus.

She woke up before dawn and the clock on her mobile told her it was 5.15 am. It was dark and cold and soon the hunger returned.

She lay back and gave herself a talking to, saying that it was not going to be easy following her dream and forcing herself to come up with a plan of action.

And as daylight began to creep under the canvas of the big top she knew what she had to do!

Again she would have to rely on her wits and tell some tall tales but if it worked, it meant the day ahead would see an improvement for her.

By the time she could hear the circus staff starting to get busy Chloe decided it was time to act and she sneaked out of her hiding place.

She was relieved to see the sun rising over the sea, meaning it should soon start to warm up a little bit.

The site was becoming a hive of activity with people crossing to and fro and Chloe took the opportunity to walk down to the beach.

The sand was soft beneath her feet and she took off her shoes and socks so she could feel it properly and she walked the length of the beach before returning to the circus site.

As she returned she saw the woman from the kiosk walking across the grass to her little room, ready to start selling tickets.

Chloe waited to give her time to settle in before making her move and putting her plan into action!

Walking in a confident manner, so people would assume she knew what she was doing and wouldn't stop her, she went to the kiosk and knocked on the door.

The young woman opened the door and said "hello again," in a cheery voice as she saw the 13-year-old waiting on the step outside.

"The boss has told me to come and give you a hand," Chloe said.

"Well, that's a first. Usually I'm left to do everything. But what about your parents, where are they? And shouldn't you be going to school?" the woman asked.

Chloe had already worked out her story. "Mum and dad have had to go to grandma's. She had a fall in the night and needs their help.

"And I'm between schools and can't start at the new one till after half term. My name's Chloe by the way," she said confidently.

The young woman seemed to accept the story. "Oh, Ok," she said.

"Well, it would be good to get some help. I need to go to the printers to pick up the new posters and start to put them up in Tingleside so if you could hold the fort that would be great.

She produced a cardboard box full of tickets and patted the top of it as she told Chloe: "If anyone arrives to buy tickets, they're here.

"My name's Rachel so let's get on with the day!" she told her new assistant. Rachel showed Chloe where the petty cash was kept if anyone needed change for their tickets and how to operate the electronic credit card machine for people who wanted to use a card or an app on their mobile phone to pay.

"Well, that's the lot for now. I'll get away to the printers and see you later.

"There's tea, coffee and biscuits over there if you want anything," Rachel said, waving her hand to the other side of the kiosk, and she set off, leaving Chloe in charge.

Chloe looked to where Rachel had pointed and found the kettle, coffee, tea bags and powdered milk and a tin full of biscuits.

"That'll have to do for breakfast," she said to herself as she put the kettle on, helped herself to a handful of biscuits and prepared to wait for any customers.

Within half an hour people started to arrive to buy tickets and Chloe served them with a smile on her face.

So far, her plan was working. But for how long could she keep it up?

Bruin suddenly stopped and tugged on his lead in the other direction, barking loudly. "

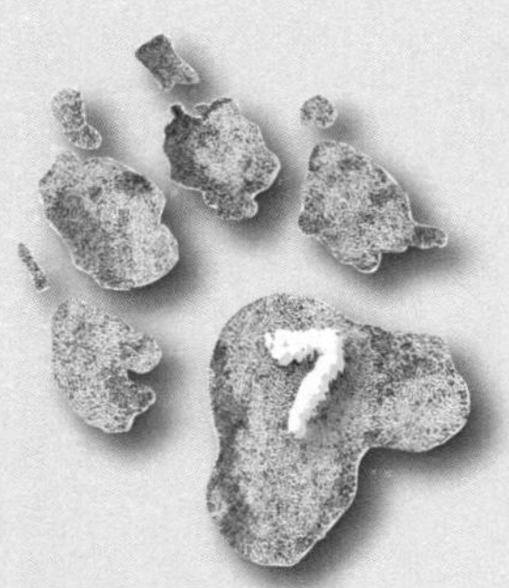

The Cat In The Tree

After all the excitement of finding the boy cut off by the tide, and then a ride in the inshore lifeboat, Bruin was happy lying in his bed the next morning.

The children had all gone to school, Mr Wilkie had gone to work and Mrs Wilkie was making a start on decorating the two birthday cakes.

She had started with the rocket cake for Jimmy and by now it was looking as realistic as possible, with a white and blue body and red fins.

For a final touch she used red and orange icing to look like flames coming from the rocket as it sped through space.

The cake was then put on a black cake board, decorated with dozens of small stars and larger planets, made of icing.

"That looks great, even if I say so myself," Mrs Wilkie said to herself.

Any seven-year-old space mad child would be thrilled to get it as a birthday cake!

The cake for Paris was proving more tricky, as she had feared.

But it was taking shape and all she had to do now was use different coloured icing for the horse and rider.

She looked at her notes which said the horse had to be chestnut coloured with four white "socks" and she experimented with different mixes until she got the right shade of light brown and started to fill in the horse shape.

Bruin liked these mornings when it was just him and Mrs Wilkie and he knew he could laze in bed as long as he wanted.

He loved the weekends too, when the children were home and there was plenty to do, but after all the activity yesterday he was very happy to have a quiet time today.

He didn't even stir when there was a knock at the door and Mrs Wilkie got up from the kitchen table and opened it to find Tom, the postman, standing there.

"Morning Mrs Wilkie," Tom said. "Got one that needs to be signed for," he explained and passed over a machine so Mrs Wilkie could write her signature on the electronic screen.

"Lovely job," said Tom as he took the machine back and handed a parcel to Mrs Wilkie. "Have a nice morning," he added as he left with a cheery wave.

Bruin still didn't move as Mrs Wilkie took the parcel back to the table and used scissors to cut through the brown tape holding it together.

"I think I know what this will be," she said to herself as the parcel started to open and she tore at the packaging.

"Ah yes, here it is," she said as she pulled out a new food mixer to replace the old one she used for her cakes but which was on its last legs.

"What a beauty!" she said excitedly as she took the mixer from its box and proudly sat it on the kitchen table.

She stood back to admire the shiny red and silver coloured machine and felt very pleased with her purchase.

Bruin had finally stirred, sitting up to see what was going on. But when he realised what all the fuss was about he decided the best thing to do was settle down again and he was soon curled up in his bed once more.

And so the day went on, with Bruin content to be busy doing nothing while Mrs Wilkie finished off both cakes.

By early afternoon she was happy that both were perfect and that all the icing was dry so she put them both in boxes and tied them with colourful ribbons.

She then put a sticker on each box "Something special to make your smile wide, from Happy Cakes of Tingleside," the stickers said.

When both boxes were ready Mrs Wilkie fetched

her coat and Bruin's lead.

"Come on lazybones, time to deliver these cakes," she said to Bruin and he slowly got to his feet and stood quietly so the lead could be easily attached.

Taking one cake at a time, Mrs Wilkie put them in the boot of her car and Bruin sat on the floor in front of the passenger seat as the car set off on its special deliveries.

Both cakes had to go to the other end of Tingleside and Mrs Wilkie decided to deliver Jimmy's first.

She pulled her car into Jimmy's road and found his house, knowing he should be at school so wouldn't see the special cake being delivered.

She parked opposite the house and told Bruin he could come too, as long as he stayed on his lead.

A minute later they were handing the cake over to Jimmy's grandmother, who was looking after his little sister, Lucy, while the childrens' parents were at work.

As they came away from the house Bruin suddenly stopped and tugged on his lead in the other direction, barking loudly.

"What is it Bruin?" Mrs Wilkie asked as Bruin continued to pull on his lead.

She followed his gaze and saw the reason for the rumpus as she spotted a black and white cat up a tree.

As Bruin continued to bark and the cat hissed at

the dog Mrs Wilkie told him "come along Bruin, leave the cat alone," and she pulled at the lead so he had to follow her back to the car.

She ordered him back inside and as he settled down again with his chin resting on the passenger seat, the car set off to take the other cake to Paris's house.

It was only 10 minutes away and the house had its own driveway so Mrs Wilkie parked there and left Bruin in the car as she fetched the cake from the boot and delivered it to Paris's mother.

Less than a minute later she was back in the car, telling Bruin "there we are, all done!"

They set off for home and the route took them back past Jimmy's house, which was close to a local shop.

"Milk and butter," Mrs Wilkie repeated to herself over and over again to make sure she didn't forget to stop to get a couple of things she needed.

She was still muttering it as she pulled in again opposite Jimmy's house and close to the shop.

"You wait here," she told Bruin as she got out and prepared to walk towards the shop.

Bruin, though, could sense something wasn't quite right and he jumped up onto the passenger seat and started whining.

"What is it Bruin?" Mrs Wilkie asked and then told him "stop being silly, I'll only be a couple of minutes."

But Bruin wouldn't settle down as he usually did

and jumped over to the driver's chair and put his paws on the edge of the window, whining even louder and looking hard in the direction of the tree.

Mrs Wilkie stood outside the car and tried to work out what Bruin was trying to tell her.

"Perhaps you need to spend a penny," she said and she opened the car door, picked up Bruin's lead and attached it to let him out.

But rather than needing to spend a penny, Bruin strained on the lead and Mrs Wilkie was forced to walk with him across the road.

Bruin stood at the bottom of the tree, scratching at the ground and looking up into the very top branches.

Mrs Wilkie stood next to him and followed his gaze up into the tree – and there, on one of the highest branches, was the cat still firmly stuck and too frightened to try to get down.

"Oh Bruin, how did you know the cat was still stuck up there?" she asked, looking up at where the cat was sitting in the branches.

Now, if you've ever seen someone looking upwards you'll know how difficult it is not to do the same, or perhaps you've been looking up at something and other people have joined you.

Well, no sooner had Mrs Wilkie started looking up than another woman came by, stopped and also looked into the tree. "Oh dear, a cat is stuck," she said as she gazed upwards.

A few seconds later an old man on his walking

stick came by and joined the two women staring up into the tree. "He's well and truly stuck," the old man said.

"If I was 50 years younger I'd climb up there and fetch him but I can't do it now," he said.

Mrs Wilkie asked, "what shall we do? Should we call the fire brigade?" The three of them continued to stand and stare and then someone else came along.

This time it was a much younger man, someone in his 20s, and he joined the small party of people looking upwards.

"It's a cat, stuck up the tree," the old man explained and Mrs Wilkie said: "We were just wondering if we should call the fire brigade."

The young man stopped gazing up into the tree and looked towards Mrs Wilkie.

"No point doing that. I'm a fireman on my way to work. I can get up there and fetch the cat," he told her.

"But isn't it dangerous to climb up there without any ropes or anything?" asked Mrs Wilkie.

"I'll be alright, it will only take few minutes," the off duty fireman said. "Good lad," said the old man. "I'd have done it if I was a lot younger. But my legs these days…"

"No worries," said the young man and he put down a rucksack he was carrying and started to climb the tree.

In less than a minute he was at the top and the small group on the ground looked on as he

But rather than being grateful for being rescued the frightened cat hissed at her rescuer and tried to get out of his arms.

reached out and picked up the cat.

But rather than being grateful for being rescued the frightened cat hissed at her rescuer and tried to get out of his arms.

The young man talked to the cat in a quiet, calm voice and stroked her head to let her know he was a friend and the cat settled down and even started to purr.

With one arm around the cat the young man began the climb back down to the ground as the onlookers called out encouragement like "well done" and "you're nearly there," until the young man reached the ground with the cat in his arms.

Everyone watching broke in to a loud round of applause.

Bruin was by now much more settled and was sitting quietly as the cat was put on the ground and ran off towards its home.

"Phew," said Mrs Wilkie as the young man put his rucksack back on. "It's a good job you came by when you did."

"My pleasure. Glad to be of service," said the young man and he went on his way.

With nothing more to see the others moved on as well and Mrs Wilkie put Bruin back in the car and went to the shop. She was still muttering "milk and butter," to herself again to make sure she remembered what she needed.

When she reached the shop she stopped to look at posters and notices in the window.

As she looked, a new poster was about to be put

up from inside the shop and it caught Mrs Wilkie's eye. The shopkeeper was standing beside a young woman, who had a roll of posters in her arms, and she passed one to be stuck into the window.

The door to the shop was open and Mrs Wilkie heard the shopkeeper saying to the young woman, "There you go Rachel, all done,"

The young woman replied "thank you Mr Roberts, that's really good of you. I'll make sure to leave two tickets on the door for you and Mrs Roberts. It's going to be a great show!"

Interested to see what the show was about, Mrs Wilkie read the poster. "Mr Pickering's Amazing Circus, for five nights only!

Tingleside beachside park October 26th to 30th."

There were pictures of circus performers and a mobile phone number for buying tickets. "Just the job for a half term treat!" Mrs Wilkie thought to herself and she took a note of the telephone number for tickets.

When she got back to the car with the shopping she told Bruin that all the excitement was over and it was time to go home.

Bruin was very pleased to hear it and was looking forward to getting back to his bed before the children returned home.

"Hmmm," Mrs Wilkie said to herself. "A trip to the circus.

What fun for all of us!"

A Policeman Visits The Circus

Dyson was still the only officer on duty at Leymouth and was at his desk looking at the list of jobs which had mounted up.

First there were the two burglaries, then the farmer who as a protest had dropped a pile of manure outside his local bank branch.

On top of that there was now a case of shoplifting and a theft from a local pub which needed looking in to.

And then there was the case of the missing girl, who might be at the circus which had just arrived in the town.

PC Dyson looked again at her file.

He read that Chloe Marsden was 13 years old and had run away from Merrymeet children's home in Berkshire, going missing on Monday morning, two days ago.

It said she had been to Mr Pickering's Amazing Circus on the Saturday night and had told friends she wanted to join the circus so he had to check if she had been spotted there.

It was now Wednesday morning and PC Dyson had a spare hour which meant he could fit in a trip to the circus to ask if anyone had seen the missing girl.

He climbed into his patrol car and made the short drive to where the circus had set up.

As he arrived it was a scene of activity, with the final ropes being tightened on the big top and people carrying equipment.

Suddenly there was a loud bang like a gunshot and PC Dyson turned quickly to where the sound had come from. "On top of everything else, what's now happening?" he wondered as he tried to work out what was going on.

The noise was like a shotgun and came from inside the big top.

The policeman gingerly pulled back a flap over the entrance to the area, frightened in case whoever had fired the shot was going to fire again. But he smiled to himself when he saw the scene inside the big top.

No-one had been shot he was pleased to see as he discovered that what he had actually heard was "Fritz the Human Cannonball" being fired from a cannon and landing on a net on the other side of the big top.

"Phew, thank goodness for that," PC Dyson said to himself as he saw Fritz bouncing on the net before doing a forward roll to get back onto the ground.

As he stood watching a man in a brightly coloured jacket and a top hat approached.

"Good morning officer, and what brings you to Mr Pickering's Amazing Circus? Nothing wrong I trust?" the man asked.

"And you are…?" PC Dyson asked in his official voice, licking the end of his short pencil and preparing to write any information in his trusty pocket notebook.

"I, sir, am Mr Oswald Pickering. Proprietor and ring master of Mr Pickering's Amazing Circus, at your service.

"How may I be of help to one of His Majesty's fine custodians of the law? Mr Pickering's Amazing Circus is always keen to help the police in any way we can," said the red faced and tubby ring master.

"I am on the lookout for a young girl who has run away from her care home and we have reason to believe she may be here, with your amazing circus.

"I have a picture here of her," said PC Dyson, reaching into his pocket to pull out the photograph of Chloe.

Mr Pickering studied the picture before saying: "I'm sorry officer. I've not seen her. Perhaps someone else here knows something of her. You are welcome to ask around."

"How many people work here at the circus?" PC Dyson asked.

"With all the circus artistes, the set builders

No-one had been shot he was pleased to see as he discovered that what he had actually heard was "Fritz the Human Cannonball" being fired from a canon and landing on a net on the other side of the big top.

and the support staff there are some 84 people in all.

"And a very happy team we are, delighting in the pleasure we bring to children and their parents wherever we go!" said Mr Pickering.

"My right hand man is Mr Holdroyd. He might know something."

With that he called out "Herbert, would you be kind enough to join us for a moment?" and a tall, skinny man approached.

"Yes Mr Pickering, what can I do for you?" Mr Holdroyd asked.

"Ah Herbert, it is not something for me but for this fine member of the local constabulary.

"Would you be good enough to explain the situation of the missing girl to Mr Holdroyd, officer?" Mr Pickering said.

PC Dyson told Mr Holdroyd about Chloe and showed him the picture but he slowly shook his head. "I'm sorry officer. I've not seen her," he said.

"Perhaps you'd be good enough to leave the picture with us and we'll show it around. Someone else might know something," said Mr Pickering.

"Yes, I was just about to suggest that. Here is my telephone number in case you have any news for me," said PC Dyson, handing over a calling card with his details.

"I must get on now, I have plenty of other cases that need my attention," and with that PC Dyson left the big top and climbed back into his car.

Meanwhile, less than 20 yards away, Chloe sat with Rachel in the kiosk as another customer bought four tickets for the circus.

She had so far spent two full nights in the big top while pretending to Rachel that she was still waiting for her parents to come back from her grandmother's house.

She was finding it hard to sleep on the wooden benches and all she had eaten was biscuits from the tin but what other choice did she have?

If she told Rachel the truth she'd surely be sent back to the children's home and her dream of becoming a circus performer like the Flying Foxes would be over.

Rachel, though, was already starting to have her doubts about Chloe's story.

How come she had seen nothing of the young girl's parents and would they really go off and leave a 13-year-old to fend for herself?

There was something fishy going on, she thought.

Determined to get to the truth, she waited until there was a lull in business before she questioned the teenager.

"Is there any news from your parents?" she asked. "Um, my mum said gran was still feeling whoozy after her fall.

She didn't know when they'd be back," said Chloe.

"And how are you looking after yourself in your caravan?"Rachel asked. "What are you having to eat?"

Chloe looked at the ground so that she avoided Rachel's eyes.

"Um, mum left meals in the freezer for me," she said, making up another story. Then she thought to herself, "If only I can get through this week I'll be able to think of something."

"Well, as long as you're alright," said Rachel, seemingly satisfied at Chloe's answers.

Then another customer called in to the kiosk to buy tickets for the circus and Chloe relaxed.

She had got away with it again… for now.

After returning to Leymouth Station later in the day PC Dyson telephoned PC Rawlings to tell her he had been to the circus to ask about Chloe.

"No-one has seen Chloe but I left a photograph of her and my details in case there was some other news," PC Dyson told her.

"They've promised to ask around and let me know if anyone has any news. I'm sorry but there's nothing else I can do," he added before putting down the telephone.

He was already thinking about the two burglaries he had to investigate.

Emma Rawlings was not surprised that PC Dyson had not had any luck with finding Chloe.

She knew he did not have time to carry out a more thorough investigation and she had no faith in anything more being done.

"I'm going to have to do some work on this myself," she thought, remembering the next place where the circus was headed.

She switched on her computer and typed "places to stay in Tingleside" into the search engine and soon it had suggestions.

Within a few minutes she had booked a visit to The Old Chapel B&B in Tingleside for the following week.

"If you want a job doing well, do it yourself," she said quietly after booking the room at the B&B. She felt excited at the prospect of trying to track down Chloe.

Her week off would give her the chance to do some investigating herself and, if nothing else, it would give her the chance to spend a few days by the seaside!

With nearly every ticket sold for the Saturday night Mr Pickering was in great form.

The Circus Arrives In Tingleside

Opening night for the circus in Leymouth was a great success. There was a good crowd cheering on the acts as they were each introduced by Mr Pickering, who waved his wooden cane and raised his top hat to give an indication of the excitement to come with each different performance.

Chloe was able to sneak in to the big top to see the show each night and afterwards stayed out of sight until the big top was empty.

She then crept back in to go to her usual spot to settle down for another chilly, uncomfortable night on the benches.

Thankfully she discovered that each night, after the public had gone, the hot dog and burger stands gave away any unsold food rather than throw it away.

It meant she was able to at least get some hot food inside her before settling down each night.

By the time of the Saturday night show – which was always the busiest night of the week- she had her routine well and truly established.

The hot dog and burger people had got to know her and always had something ready for when she arrived at their stalls.

Thankfully for her, they had not been shown the photograph of the missing girl and they just accepted her story of being at the circus with her parents and helping out with selling tickets.

On some evenings, if she was lucky, there was even some left over milkshake and, as a real treat, the candy floss seller would sometimes have a bag left over which she could have as a sort of pudding.

It wasn't the healthiest diet in the world but at least it was food, Chloe thought as she tucked in each night.

With nearly every ticket sold for the Saturday night Mr Pickering was in great form.

He whipped up the excitement levels and told his corny jokes about the trapeze artists being in the swing of things and one of the clowns feeling sad because he had banged his funny bone.

The audience loved the show and as they filed out they were all talking noisely about their favourite bits.

Chloe listened to the happy customers but she felt worried about having to hide again the next morning as the circus was packed up ready to move on to its next destination.

And then, next week, she would have to convince Rachel again that her parents were still with her grandmother but would be back soon.

As she tucked in to her latest feast of hot dog, burger and candy floss, Chloe started to make plans for when the big top was being taken down in the morning.

She knew she would have to repeat what she had done on the morning when she first ran away to the circus.

That meant hiding on one of the benches and then staying out of sight until the lorries pulled in to their next destination.

But before that, all through Sunday she had to stay out of the way as the big top was being taken down and put onto lorries.

As darkness fell she sneaked back to the circus and again found a loose bit of rope on one of the canvases.

"Thank goodness for Tony," she thought to herself, remembering the new member of staff who was sloppy at tying the ropes as tightly as he should.

She again sneaked under the canvas and up to where she could try to make herself as comfortable as possible.

She had a restless and cold night as she waited for dawn when the team would again do their checks before setting off.

Sure enough, they found the loose bit of rope and blamed Tony for again not doing a thorough job and it was properly tightened before the lorries set off.

Chloe kept hidden while the lorries pulled away. The journey this time was a lot shorter and it was less than two hours before Chloe's lorry was parked.

Once again the workers went for breakfast after loosening the covers and Chloe sneaked out to look about her.

As she came into the fresh air she noticed a sign telling her the circus was parked close to the beach at the next destination for the show – a place called Tingleside.

Chloe had never heard of Tingleside but she thought it looked a nice place, with the beach stretching into the distance with acres of golden sand and rocks at either end.

She also noticed a beach café called Salvino's and saw the circus workmen sitting on tables in the early morning sunshine as they waited for their breakfast.

But despite the lovely views, Chloe felt lonely and unsure of her future.

She saw families walking on the beach, most of them with their dogs, and she wondered how she was going to get through another week telling stories and fibs about her made up parents still visiting her made up grandma.

There would also be days of eating nothing but biscuits from the tin before the burger, hot dog and candy floss stalls were set up again.

Nights would be spent sleeping on the hard wooden bench but to Chloe it was worth it.

All she wanted was to one day become a real part of the circus team.

She would then have a comfortable bed in one of the caravans, a good breakfast every morning and a proper dinner each night.

But how could she get that? She felt that Rachel already doubted her tales and no-one else at the circus even knew she was there.

She thought about Tilly and Megan having breakfast at Merrymeet and then playing in the large garden or going out for a bike ride.

She knew it was half term which meant a lot of fun all week with the children taken for outings and special treats.

But for Chloe there would be none of that, just hiding and hoping not to be found out for another week.

She couldn't stop a tear welling up in her eyes and trickling down her cheeks.

She still believed she was doing the right thing in following her dream and even though it was a lot tougher than she had imagined she had to carry on.

Emma had spoken again to the staff at Merrymeet in case they had heard from Chloe (which they hadn't) and told them of her plan to go to Tingleside on her week off.

They had wished her luck in finding Chloe and also provided one of her jumpers, which Emma said would be useful if the local police dog team was able to help track Chloe down.

"Tell her we miss her if you find her," Tilly and Megan told Emma and they had both written letters which could be given to their friend if she was found.

"I'm going to do my best to find Chloe and make sure she's safe and well," Emma promised the girls and the staff at Merrymeet before going off duty and preparing for her trip away.

At the Wilkies' house half term meant a late start to the morning, which suited Bruin who was able to have a lie-in and properly relax.

But although the children had the week off, their parents were both still working and Mr Wilkie had to get off to his office and Mrs Wilkie still had more birthday cakes to make and deliver.

She also had her first order that year for a Christmas cake for a family in the town who wanted a cake big enough for 14 people to all tuck in.

By the time the children were all down for breakfast Bruin was up and welcomed each of them with a wagging tail and friendly lick.

They all had cereal bowls in front of them and a box of Frosties was produced as a half term breakfast treat. Mrs Wilkie then said she had another piece of exciting news.

"Are we getting a new pet?" Henry asked but Harriet told him: "We don't need another pet,

Bruin is the best pet anyone could have."

She then turned to her mother and asked "are you making us a special cake?"

Mrs Wilkie told the children "it's not a new pet and it's not a special cake.

"We're having a special outing... we're going to the circus!"

The children all burst into excited applause. "Fantastic," said Florence. "We've never been to the circus. It's going to be great fun. When are we going?"

Mrs Wilkie told them: "I've ordered the tickets for Friday night but we have to go there before Wednesday to pick them up.

"It's at beachside so we can call in while we're taking Bruin to the beach for some exercise."

"Wow," said Harriet. "That really is exciting. What a great week we have coming up!"

Mrs Wilkie agreed. "It's going to be a proper family treat.

" I saw a poster for the circus while I was out delivering cakes and I thought straight away that we should go.

"But before then I'm going to be quite busy making cakes so you can have lots of fun with Bruin for the week."

As soon as breakfast was over the children and Bruin went into the sitting room and started to plan for their first ever trip to the circus.

Henry said he was looking forward to the clowns

but Florence and Harriet wanted to see the trapeze artists the most; one thing was for sure, there would be something for everyone.

Emma Rawlings arrived at Tingleside later that afternoon and her car's sat nav took her straight to Porter Street where The Old Chapel B&B was situated.

As she unloaded her bags she had her first look at Tingleside.

It was a busy little town and Emma received a very warm welcome from Mrs Huntley, who ran the B&B.

The landlady showed Emma to her room with two single beds and a window overlooking the garden and, in the distance, she could glimpse the sea.

"Oh, this will be perfect," said Emma as she sat on the edge of one of the beds.

"Are you down for a holiday or perhaps on business?" asked Mrs Huntley.

Emma didn't want to say

anything about looking for a runaway from a children's home so she just said "Just a short break for a few days.

"I have the week off work and thought that spending some of the time here would be perfect. I'm looking forward to some nice walks on the beach."

"That will be lovely, the weather forecast is good for the week and being half term there's plenty going on," said Mrs Huntley.

"That sounds great," said Emma. "I saw a poster saying the circus was in town?"

"Yes, they turned up earlier this morning and will be setting up in the park next to the beach.

"It should be a good show and I'm planning to take my two grandchildren there later in the week," said Mrs Huntley.

She then left the room telling Emma to come and find her if she needed anything.

On the sideboard there were pamphlets showing various local attractions.

These included some caves, a small theme park, a water park and an animal rescue centre.

There was also a leaflet for Mr Pickering's Amazing Circus with details on the back of the times of shows that week.

The opening night was Wednesday and then shows every evening until Saturday, with an extra performance on Saturday afternoon.

There was a mobile phone number for ordering tickets. Emma thought about calling but decided it would be better to take a wander to Beachside Park.

That would give her a chance to have a look at the circus being set up before starting her investigation into Chloe's disappearance.

She felt happy with her decision to come to Tingleside and use her week off to find Chloe, knowing that people at the children's home were relying on her to make sure Chloe was safe and well.

But what if Chloe didn't want to go back? Emma thought to herself.

She would have to hand the case over to social services and goodness knows where Chloe would end up. The whole situation was a worry for the young police constable.

"We'll just have to cross that bridge when we come to it," Chloe said to herself before making a start on unpacking her bags and then settling down with a cup of tea and some biscuits on one of the comfy looking chairs by the window.

As the afternoon turned into evening activity at the circus started to come to a close.

Rachel had been running the sales kiosk all afternoon and was glad of the help when Chloe turned up at lunchtime to give a hand.

Being half term it was sure to be a busy week and quite a few of the people buying tickets were down in Tingleside on holiday.

So, with them and the local families, it was going to be good for business and as well as visitors to the kiosk the mobile phone for the ticket line was ringing regularly.

Rachel had planned to question Chloe again about her parents and when they would be back with the circus but it had been so busy she had not had a chance.

So when it came time to close the kiosk for the day Rachel asked Chloe if she could help again the next day, which was sure to be just as busy.

"Of course, being half term this will be the last week you can help. Didn't you say you were starting at a new school after half term?" Rachel asked.

Chloe couldn't think of any new excuse to make up about not going to school so she just muttered, "yes, that's right" and thought to herself that she would have to come up with a new story for next week.

"Well, goodnight and thanks for your help," Rachel said as she locked up the kiosk and prepared to head for her comfortable caravan.

According to what Chloe had been saying, she should also be heading for a warm and cosy caravan.

But the reality was all she had to look forward to there was another horrible night on the wooden benches and trying not to be spotted.

"Can we go to get the circus tickets today?" he asked hopefully. "That's what we were just talking about," said Harriet.
FLORENCE
HARRIET
TRAIN YOUR DOG
1 FETCH
2 SIT
3 FIND
4 LIE DOWN

PC Rawlings Starts Her Investigation

Florence and Harriet were both awake fairly early on Tuesday morning, even though there was no school to go to.

Henry, who had been lying still and quiet on his bed for at least half an hour, heard his sisters chatting and decided it was safe to go in to their bedroom without being shouted at to "get out!"

Henry gently pushed their bedroom door half open and asked "are you awake?" to make sure.

He was greeted cheerfully by the girls, who both said, "yes, come on in," so he opened the door some more and walked in.

"Can we go to get the circus tickets today?" he asked hopefully. "That's what we were just talking about," said Harriet.

"I think mummy will be too busy to come as well but hopefully they'll give us the tickets. We're going to go down there this morning."

"Great," said Henry. "We'll take Bruin for a run

on the beach at the same time."

The children decided they would get dressed and head off as soon as possible.

Just 10 minutes later they were downstairs and tucking into Frosties.

Bruin had climbed out of his bed to say good morning but was now curled up again.

He knew, though, from the excited young voices that a trip to the beach was being planned.

Emma slept soundly in the comfortable bed at The Old Chapel and over breakfast chatted with two other guests.

They told her they were going to spend the day exploring the town centre.

"We might get down to the beach in the afternoon. I've heard there's a good café overlooking the sea," said the husband.

Emma, though, wouldn't be spending her time sight-seeing.

Instead she planned to make a start on her investigation looking for Chloe.

She didn't say anything about what she would be up to and said to the other couple "have a lovely day," as she went back to her room to prepare for going out.

She packed the jumper belonging to Chloe in her bag and decided she would go later to the local police station to meet their dog team if she thought she would need their help.

She set off on foot for the beachside park,

leaving her car at the B&B, and within 10 minutes had arrived to see the finishing touches being put to the circus tent.

She could hear a band practicing inside, ready to accompany the acts with dramatic or comical music.

Emma walked right around the outside of the big top and there was a real sense of excitement, with final preparations before opening night.

She saw one of the workmen checking that the ropes holding up the big top were tight enough and, when he had stopped, she approached him and asked if he'd seen a young girl, showing him Chloe's picture.

The man studied the photograph before shaking his head and saying he hadn't seen her.

He called over two other circus workers and they both said the same thing – there had been no sighting of Chloe.

Emma was not put off though.

She knew that if Chloe was with the circus she would have been doing her best to not be noticed.

But surely the time would come when she would have to make herself known to someone.

"But what if she's not here at all?" Emma thought to herself before telling herself off. "Stop thinking like that. You've only just started!" she said beneath her breath.

She walked again around the outside of the big top, stopping every now and again to show someone Chloe's picture and asking if they had seen her.

But no-one had seen anything of the missing girl and someone suggested speaking to Mr Pickering himself and told her where she could find him inside the big top.

She pulled back the canvas cover over the entrance and entered the big top just as two jugglers were starting to rehearse their act.

Emma watched for a few moments as they went through their routine, which included tossing flaming sticks to each other.

"Wow, what an act," thought Emma as they finished and someone she assumed was Mr Pickering shouted to them "well done, well done. An excellent performance. The crowd will be delighted!"

As Emma approached Mr Pickering he turned to face her.

"Ah, young lady. Can I be of assistance? Mr Pickering at your service!"

"Good morning Mr Pickering and I'm sorry to trouble you.

"But I wonder if you might be able to help. I'm looking for someone who might he here at your circus," said Emma.

She produced the photograph and explained about Chloe going missing and that she was a police officer from her local area.

"Well, let me think. A policeman at Leymouth asked me the same thing and I had to tell him I hadn't seen her.

"I asked around but no-one had spotted her. Why are you so sure she's here at the circus?" Mr Pickering said.

"That's the trouble," said Emma. "We're not sure she is here.

"But she had told her friends she wanted to join the circus so I've come down to see if she can be found.

"First of all I want to make sure she is safe and well, that's the main thing," she said.

"Yes indeed, that is the most important thing. I hope you manage to find her," said Mr Pickering.

She thanked Mr Pickering for his help and left the big top, noticing a queue of people outside the sales kiosk nearby and wondering if she should buy a ticket for opening night.

She decided to join the queue and checked that she had her purse with her so she could buy a ticket for the show.

But just as she opened her handbag and pulled out her purse she was shocked to see two men come face to face with her.

"We'll take that," said one of the rough looking men, who immediately snatched Emma's purse and the pair of them ran off.

"Hey, stop," shouted Emma as the two men raced away. Her purse contained all her cash for her B&B room.

People in the queue turned to see what was

going on and all Emma could do was gasp "they've stolen my purse," as the two robbers raced away.

Quickly she decided she had to do something and started to run after the pair, who by now were at least 50 metres ahead of her.

She saw them jump over a small fence at the edge of the park and then they were on the long stretch of gravel between the park and the beach.

"Stop, stop," shouted Emma but the pair took no notice and carried on running away.

Florence, Harriet and Henry were walking back from the beach with Bruin when suddenly they were nearly knocked over by the two thieves.

A few seconds later a young woman ran past them, clearly chasing the pair and still calling for them to stop.

"They've got my purse," Emma shouted as she saw a group of men who she hoped might help catch the thieves.

But they did nothing to help and just carried on walking towards the beach.

The Wilkie children and Bruin though decided to take action. "They've stolen her purse," said Florence and Bruin started to strain on his lead as if to say "let me at them!"

"Alright Bruin, get the purse back," Florence said to him and she unclipped his lead.

Bruin knew exactly what was needed and straight away he set off after the men.

He ran past Emma as she raced after the thieves and a few seconds later he was right behind the thieves.

Now, a police dog is trained to catch running away thieves by jumping up and grabbing an arm with their teeth.

But Bruin never got to that part of his training before he went to live his new family.

So as he closed in on the pair of them he decided on his own method of stopping them.

They were both running as fast as they could but Bruin got right behind one of them and then put down his nose and gave a nudge to the running man's foot.

It was enough to send him tumbling forwards and as he did so he fell into the other thief and he also lost his balance and fell to the ground.

Both thieves ended up one on top of the other and Bruin ran to the other side of them and growled as loud as he could to stop them getting back up and running off again.

Very soon afterwards Emma joined them and grabbed her purse out of the hand of one of the thieves.

"I'm a police officer and you're both under arrest," she told them.

She used her mobile phone to call the local police station and very soon a patrol car turned up. Emma explained what had happened and both men were taken away.

"We've been after this pair for a few weeks,"

Bruin put down his nose and gave a nudge to the running man's foot. It was enough to send him tumbling forwards and as he did so he fell into the other thief and he also lost his balance and fell to the ground.

the policeman said as the men were bundled into the back of the patrol car.

"They turned up in Tingleside last month and since then they've been snatching handbags and purses all over town.

"It's good that they've been caught before moving on to the next town and doing the same thing there."

By now the three children who owned the dog had arrived at the scene.

"Your dog did a brilliant job. What's his name?" asked Emma and Harriet told her it was Bruin.

"What a great dog. He's just like the German Shepherds at our station," Emma told the three children.

"I'm a police officer but I'm on holiday this week. I didn't expect something like that to happen on my first day!"

The older of the two girls told her, "Bruin was actually bred to be a police dog but was too sleepy and too friendly so we were allowed to adopt him. We love him to bits."

Then the younger girl, who was holding on to the lead, said: "Even though he didn't finish his training to be a police dog he can't help getting involved in exciting things.

"He's already done two rescues. He saved an old lady who had had a fall at her home and before that he tracked down Henry here when he went missing," pointing to the young boy who was with them.

"And don't forget about the boy cut off by the tide. Bruin saved him as well," said Henry.

"So he's good at tracking is he?" asked Emma, starting to think of a plan.

"It just so happens that I'm trying to find a missing girl. I've got one of her jumpers with me. I wonder if Bruin would mind seeing if he can help find her?"

"Oh yes," cried Henry excitedly. "Bruin will find her, he's brilliant at tracking. Please let us help."

Emma looked at the older girls and Harriet said she was sure Bruin wouldn't mind giving it a go.

"Absolutely," said Florence. "If anyone can find her, Bruin can!"

Emma pulled Chloe's jumper out of her bag. "This belongs to the missing girl. Her name is Chloe and we believe she may have run away to join the circus.

"But no-one I've spoken to has seen her so I'm not even sure that she is here," she said.

She put the jumper under Bruin's nose and he gave it a good sniff and then started to sniff the ground, trying to pick up a trail.

"Thanks for helping. It will be wonderful if Bruin can find Chloe for us," said Emma.

The queue at the sales kiosk had by now disappeared and Rachel sighed as she managed to have a moment's rest before the next people turned up to buy tickets.

It was looking like being one of the busiest

weeks of the year and she knew Mr Pickering would be thrilled when she told him how many tickets they had already sold.

"What a busy morning we've had," Rachel said to Chloe. "I think we deserve a reward… do you like ice cream?"

Chloe said that of course she did and Rachel pulled out a £10 note from her purse and told Chloe to go and get them a double 99 each from Salvinos café.

Chloe said cheerfully "will do" and took the £10 note and left the kiosk just as Bruin was starting to track her scent from earlier, discovering that it led towards the kiosk.

As Chloe set off for Salvinos she noticed three children with a German Shepherd dog and a young woman.

As she walked towards the café she passed the children and suddenly the dog came towards her, panting and pulling on his lead, which Florence was now holding.

The children at once suspected that Bruin had found the missing girl and Florence asked: "Is your name Chloe by any chance?"

The girl looked shocked to hear her name. "How do you know my name?" she asked.

"Because Bruin has found you," said Henry excitedly and Emma, hearing the conversation, came straight over to them.

"This is Chloe," Florence proudly told Emma.

Chloe knew the game was up. Staring at the ground she slowly nodded her head.

Emma smiled as she looked at the young girl.

Chloe's Plan Of Action

Emma stood right next to Chloe, unable to believe she was finally beside the young girl who had disappeared two weeks earlier, from the children's home.

"Are you Chloe Marsden?" she asked, just to make sure although she recognised her straight away from her photograph.

Chloe knew the game was up. Staring at the ground she slowly nodded her head.

Emma smiled as she looked at the young girl.

Then she said: "Oh Chloe, you can't believe how pleased I am to meet you."

Chloe looked up, confused. "Who are you?" she asked.

"I'm a police officer who has been looking for you since the morning you ran away. That's why I'm so pleased to see that you're safe and well.

"Everyone is so worried about you and just

wants to know that you are all right and safe, " said Emma.

Rachel, inside the kiosk, could hear the commotion outside and went to investigate.

What's going on?" she asked. "Chloe has been helping me while her parents are away looking after her grandma," Rachel said.

Chloe looked at the ground again, embarrassed to be found out after making up her stories.

"Well, I'm sorry to tell you that's not really true, is it Chloe?" Emma said.

Rachel looked at Chloe and asked her: "Is that right, Chloe? Is that not the truth?"

Chloe remained quiet as her eyes again filled with tears then said quietly "I'm sorry Rachel."

Bruin could sense how upset Chloe was and he went to her and gently nuzzled against her leg.

She crouched down and wrapped her arms around him, which brought her a lot of comfort.

Emma walked across to be next to Chloe and told her: "Don't worry Chloe. The most important thing is that you're ok.

"Tilly and Megan and everyone at Merrymeet will be so pleased to know that you're safe."

Chloe looked up at Emma and asked her: "Have you seen Tilly and Megan? How are they?"

Emma told Chloe they were both very well and had asked her to pass on the news that they were missing their friend and had written letters for her.

Chloe looked at Emma and then Rachel and started to explain what had been going on.

"All I wanted was to join the circus and become a trapeze artist. I didn't want to cause all this trouble," she said.

Rachel could see how upset the teenager was and she said gently "I understand Chloe. But there's a right way and a wrong way to go about joining the circus. Where have you been sleeping all this time?"

"In the big top. I've been hiding," Chloe said.

"But that must have been horrid. And what about your parents?"

"I'm an orphan. I've been living in a children's home," she admitted.

"I made up the stories about my parents and my grandma.

I'm really sorry," said Chloe quietly.

Rachel smiled and then rubbed Chloe's arm as if to say "I forgive you" and Emma said: "Shall we go inside Chloe and have a proper chat?" Chloe agreed and the two of them went into the kiosk.

Bruin and the children were left outside with Rachel and Harriet was the first to speak. "We only came down to collect our tickets for Friday night and look at the drama we've walked in to!"

A few minutes later Emma and Chloe came out of the kiosk.

"Everything is fine and Chloe is glad she doesn't have to carry on sleeping in the big top and lying to Rachel," said Emma.

"Thanks to Bruin she has been found before anything nasty happened to her."

"But what about our tickets?" Henry asked and Rachel was quick to tell him: "They're right inside," and said she would hand over the five tickets for the family once she went back into the kiosk.

She explained how Chloe had made up the story about her parents and grandma.

"But I can't be angry with her, she's actually been very helpful and I'll miss her.

"Chloe's had an adventure but it's time for her to be properly looked after," she said.

Chloe was looking much brighter after her chat with Emma and the first thing she did was go straight to Bruin and again cuddle his neck.

"Oh Bruin," she said. "I'm glad you found me! Everything's going to be all right!"

"What have you decided? What's going on?" Rachel asked and Emma told her: "We've spoken to everyone at Merrymeet and they're delighted Chloe has been found.

"And she doesn't need to sleep in the big top any more and eat nothing but biscuits.

"We're going for a slap up meal at the local pizza restaurant this evening and then Chloe is going to have the spare bed at my B&B so she can have a really good sleep.

"And we'd like to buy two tickets to see the

circus...which night are you going?" Emma asked the children.

"We're going on Friday night. We can't wait," said Florence.

"So two tickets for Friday night please Rachel!" said Emma.

"And Chloe has something she'd like to say to you as well."

Chloe looked shy so Emma told her, "go ahead Chloe, tell Rachel what you'd like to say." Chloe looked at Rachel, knowing how much her kindness had meant to her.

"Rachel, I'd like to say thank you for letting me join you in the kiosk and I'd like to say sorry for telling fibs rather than telling you the truth from the start.

"I've realised now that I need to do things in the right way so I'm going back to school and will do my GCSEs.

"After that I'm going to go to circus school to learn properly how to be a trapeze artist, like the Flying Foxes," said Chloe.

Rachel smiled and told Chloe, "Thank you for being so honest now and going to circus school when you're a bit older is a great idea.

"But how am I going to cope without you? you've been such a great help!"

Emma had an answer for Rachel, "We've talked about that and we'll be in Tingleside for the rest of the week.

"If you'll have her, Chloe would love to come and help you until we go back on Saturday."

"That would be fantastic," said Rachel. "And to say thank you I'll get you to meet our trapeze artists the Flying Foxes.

"They can give you loads of advice on how to join the circus – but doing it in the right way this time!"

Chloe had a beaming smile at the news and said to Rachel, "well, I've still got that £10 note to go and buy two double 99s.

"Then I'll give you a hand this afternoon before we go for a lovely pizza and then a proper night's sleep at the B&B."

"That's great," said Rachel before turning to the children and telling them "and you've got tickets to collect for Friday night's show."

The children and Bruin went into the kiosk to collect the tickets and left their home telephone number in case anyone needed to get in touch.

Then they headed down to the beach to give Bruin another good run.

On the way they spotted Chloe bringing the ice creams for her and Rachel and they waved and smiled to each other.

Chloe was looking much happier than she had when they first saw her.

"I think everything is going to be alright," Harriet said to Florence and Henry. "And it's thanks to Bruin for tracking down Chloe so quickly. He's a real superstar!"

A Night At The Circus!

When they had arrived home the children told their mother all about finding Chloe and about her plans to go to circus school and that she and Emma would also be going to the circus on Friday.

"I don't know," said Mrs Wilkie. "You can't help but have adventures when you go out with Bruin. Whatever next I wonder?"

For now it was time to settle down for the afternoon. It was the first day of half term and the children were keen to make plans for what to do before Friday.

The first thing they did was call Jasmine and invite her over and then tell her all about the latest adventure.

"What a shame I missed all the excitement," said Jasmine as she sat with the children and Bruin that afternoon.

"Oh, I'm sure there will be plenty more to come," said Florence.

For the rest of the week, Bruin was taken on walks to the beach and to the park and the children joined their mother when she went delivering cakes on the Thursday.

The only excitement was when Bruin found a hedgehog and had his nose scratched when he went to investigate what it was.

The only excitement was when Bruin found a hedgehog and had his nose scratched when he went to investigate what it was.

Soon it was Friday and Mr Wilkie made sure he was home early so they could all have dinner together before going to the circus.

Bruin was taken out earlier in the day and he was happy to stay behind and have an early night as the family went off for the evening.

They decided to drive to Beachside because it would be dark when they came home so they all piled into the car for the short journey to Beachside Park.

As they arrived there was great excitement with hundreds of people coming to see the circus.

Among them were Emma and Chloe and it was Harriet who spotted them first, running up to them to say hello.

"Come and meet mummy and daddy, we've told them all about you," said Harriet and a few seconds later they were all together and queuing up with everyone else to get in to the circus.

"We're delighted to meet you," said Mrs Wilkie. "And I understand you're planning to go to circus school after you have done your GCSEs," she said to Chloe.

"Yes, that's right. I'm going back to school but I haven't given up my dream of joining the circus.

"I met the Flying Foxes yesterday and they've told me which circus school they went to and I want to go to the same one," she said excitedly.

"It was lovely to meet them and I feel I've made so many friends here at the circus. I even met Mr Pickering and Giuseppe the clown.

"It's been a great week but the best bit has been meeting you all and Bruin of course and meeting Emma.

"I've slept in a proper bed all week and had lovely breakfasts and dinners," said Chloe.

Emma said she had also had a lovely week in Tingleside and was so pleased with the way everything had worked out.

She was telling them all about a trip she had made to the animal rescue centre and another to a craft centre while Chloe had been busy helping Rachel.

Then they arrived at the gate and it was time to take their seats for the show.

Within a few minutes of them sitting down the lights dimmed and a giant spotlight shone on Mr Pickering as he welcomed everyone to the show.

It was a complete sell out and he said it had been the best week of the year for the circus, so he thanked all the people who had come to see the performances.

Fritz the Human Cannonball was the first act and the crowd gasped as he was fired from a giant cannon and landed on the net at the other side of the circus ring.

After him came jugglers, clowns and a plate spinning act which had a great round of applause, followed by laughter as one of the plates wobbled and then smashed on the ground.

The plate spinner couldn't understand what had gone wrong – it had worked every other night.

He stood next to the wobbly pole and scratched his head, trying to work out what the problem could be.

But then he saw a length of thin cotton tied to the pole the plate was on.

He picked up the cotton thread and followed it to the edge of the ring - and guess who he found holding the other end, laughing as he did an impression of the wobbly plate, making his legs like jelly?

It was Giuseppe the clown and he chuckled as he showed the audience how he had pulled on the cotton to make the pole wobble and the plate crash to the ground.

The plate spinner saw what had happened and, after waving his fist at the naughty clown, he chased Giuseppe off to laughs and cheers from the audience.

Then it was time for the Flying Foxes and Chloe leant forward as the two girls appeared in the ring in their glamorous costumes.

Mr Pickering introduced them but then made a special announcement.

"Ladies and gentlemen, boys and girls, we have a special person in the audience tonight," he said.

"Her name is Chloe and one day we hope she will be joining our circus as a trapeze artist.

"So please stand up Chloe and let's all give her a huge Pickering circus style round of applause!" he said.

Chloe felt shy as she stood up and a spotlight

The Flying Foxes were truly magnificent and the crowd made lots of "oohs" and "aaahs" as they flew through the air.

was shone on her but she waved to the crowd while everyone clapped.

As she sat down again Emma said to her, "well you didn't expect that did you...We'll have to make doubly sure you get to circus school now!" and she gave Chloe a big hug.

The Flying Foxes were truly magnificent and the crowd made lots of "ooohs" and "aaahs" as they flew through the air.

Chloe couldn't take her eyes of the performance and Emma felt really happy to see her so excited and delighted at the show.

After their act it was more clowns and then the acrobats and the crowd burst into loud applause at the thrilling performances.

Mr Pickering was busy introducing all the acts and at the end of the show he thanked all the people for coming as the different acts did a tour of the ring to loud clapping and cheering.

"What a great night," said Mr Wilkie as the family joined the crowd leaving the big top.

Henry was way past his bedtime and was sleepily given a piggyback to the car.

The family said goodnight to Emma and Chloe and asked them to keep in touch, which they promised to do and then it was home and time for bed.

The next morning Emma prepared to drive Chloe back to Merrymeet but first Chloe asked if she could go and say a special goodbye to Rachel and then Bruin.

They went to the booking kiosk and there was a tearful goodbye as Chloe's adventure came to a close, with a promise that she would let Rachel know how things went at circus school.

"Thank you for all your work Chloe. I really look forward to hearing all your news. In the meantime it will be back to doing everything myself," said Rachel.

Emma and Chloe then went to the Wilkie house where Mrs Wilkie was putting the finishing touches to another cake.

"I just wanted to say goodbye and thank you to Bruin," said Chloe.

She went through to the kitchen where Bruin was curled up in his bed.

Kneeling down beside him, she put her arms around Bruin's neck and was given a friendly lick in return.

"Everything has worked out really well thanks to you spotting me. I owe you so much," Chloe told Bruin before it was time for her and Emma to set off in the car.

Three hours later they pulled in to the car park at Merrymeet and Tilly and Megan came running out to meet Chloe.

The staff were all there to welcome her back and to say thank you to Emma who felt proud at finding Chloe and bringing her home.

She had photographs of Bruin and the children and she showed them to Miss Hargreaves and the others as she explained their part in finding

Chloe. Then it was time for Emma to go home. The first thing she did was collect her cat, Jasper, from a neighbour.

Jasper was pleased to see her and the pair of them sat on her sofa, with Emma thinking how quiet it was to be all by herself again.

She couldn't stop thinking about her sister, Susan, who had died so young.

She still missed Susan but a plan had started to form in her mind and she smiled to herself, hoping it could be put into action...

Jasper was pleased to see her and the pair of them sat on her sofa, with Emma thinking how quiet it was to be all by herself again.

Three Months Later

It was mid January and the Wilkie family had been stuck inside for days as a snowstorm made it impossible to use the roads or even walk safely on the pavement.

The children were playing Operation, Mrs Wilkie was baking and Mr Wilkie was working from home when the telephone rang.

"I'll get it," shouted Harriet as she raced to the telephone in the hall and the rest of the family then heard her say, "oh, hello Emma. Yes, mummy is here, I'll just get her for you."

Mrs Wilkie came to the telephone and the young policewoman told her she had some exciting news for all of you.

"Oh, I can't wait to hear it and then tell all the family," said Mrs Wilkie.

"Well," said Emma. "Things have moved on a bit here and I now have someone living in the house with me."

"Oh really, and who's that?" asked Mrs Wilkie.

"It's Chloe," Emma said. "I've fostered her so she can live here but still go to the same school and see all her friends from Merrymeet whenever she wants to.

"She's been here for a month already and we're getting on really well so I'm going to properly adopt her.

"But she's more like a younger sister than a daughter and it's working really well for both of us," said Emma.

"That's wonderful news," said Mrs Wilkie. "It sounds like a really good arrangement for both of you."

"Yes, it is," said Emma. "Chloe is as determined as ever to join the circus so we've been to see the circus school which the Flying Foxes went to and she'll be going there after doing her GCSEs.

"It's all been very exciting. Everything is fine and Chloe is very happy," Emma went on.

"I love having her here and she's just like a new little sister for me. I can't believe how much has happened since Bruin found Chloe for us. He's such a clever dog!"

"He certainly is. He's full of surprises," said Mrs Wilkie. "I can't wait to tell the children all your news. They'll be very excited."

As soon as she said goodbye to Emma the children ran from the sitting room and gathered around their mother as she gave them the news.

"It's all worked out really well. And it's all

thanks to Bruin and his brilliant sense of smell that Chloe was found so quickly.

"He has proved once again that he is a very special dog," Mrs Wilkie said. Everyone was quick to agree that having Bruin as a pet was indeed the best thing that had ever happened to the Wilkie family.

"He's made such a difference to all of us and that's why we love him so much," said Harriet.

The snow continued to fall outside and the family all gathered around the crackling log fire. The children were brought a plate of crumpets with strawberry jam and there was a special dog treat for Bruin.

And as they settled down to their tea Florence looked adoringly at Bruin.

"Whatever next?" she wondered to herself.

One thing was for sure - there were more adventures to come for the dog who was too friendly to join the police but was proving a real hero to everyone who met him!

The snow continued to fall outside and the family all gathered around the crackling log fire.

Photography © Charlie Hudson: Nala

About The Author

Michael Fleet is a retired journalist living in Cornwall where he ran a B&B with his wife, Babs.

He has four grandchildren – three girls and one boy –and decided to create the Bruin adventure series after reading about an award winning police dog in Germany which had been retired and given to a family as a pet after becoming too friendly and lovable.

Photography © Michael Fleet – his own dog Maisie

How to train to join a circus!

Circus life can be great fun but also a lot of hard work and some danger for those who take their acts high above the ground in the Big Top.

Any children who dream of joining the circus are advised not to do what Chloe did and run away from home but to go to circus school to learn the skills needed to perform.

In Britain the largest circus school is Circomedia in Bristol where students learn all the circus skills from juggling through to flying on a trapeze wire. Rod Laver, a lecturer at the college and professional juggler, said the school teaches students a variety of skills so they can have full time careers in the circus.

"I have been doing my juggling act for 30 years and never get bored with it. How can you get bored of hearing the laughs, cheers and claps of the audience? It is a great life," he said.

But even before circus school there are basic skills that can be learnt to get someone ready for a life in one of the many travelling circuses around Britain and the world.

Kaya, who is what is known as an "aerialist" in Circus Funtasia was a dancer before joining the circus and she said that dancing and gymnastics were good things to practice for anyone wanting a job in the circus.

"I didn't join the circus till I was 20 but others join younger, often straight from circus school," said Kaya, who performs on a ring and on ropes high above the ground.

She said some did their act attached to a harness in case they fell off but she did not use one of them or even a safety net. "Thankfully I've never had a fall but I have known a lot of people who have. It is always a risk but it is a great life, travelling the country and meeting lots of people," said Kaya who lives in a touring caravan with her pet dog.

She loves to hear families cheering as she performs her act and loves the feeling she gets from doing her dangerous moves. "It is not for everyone but if you love adventure and excitement it is a great life," said Kaya.

Photography © Michael Fleet – 'Kaya'

www.circusfuntasia.co.uk

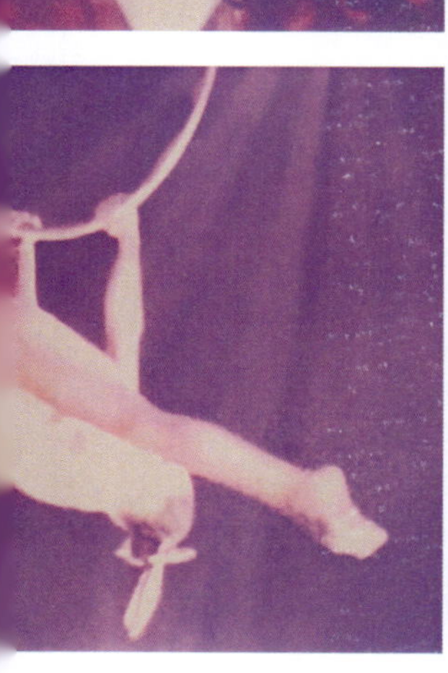

How to ADOPT a Retired Police Dog?

It is possible to give a home to one of the dozens of police dogs who retire each year or to those, like Bruin, who begin their training but are not suited to a life in the police force.

Some of these may have a physical problem, such as weak hips or other joints, while others will just not have the determination or character needed by the police. And most of these are similar to Bruin in that they are just too gentle for a career in the police!

For anyone looking to adopt a "too nice" police dog or one which has retired at the end of its career the best thing to do is contact your local police dog handling team and register your interest.

The police screen all applicants to make sure they are up to the job of looking after one of these very special dogs and, if an animal becomes available, people on the waiting list will be contacted.

Some owners of retired police dogs are supported by charities which raise money to help with vets bills as these dogs are often not able to be insured and these groups help raise awareness of the need for homes for the dogs.

In England one such charity is WAGS Retired Police Dogs, which supports police dogs from Wiltshire, Avon, Gloucestershire and Somerset and a proportion of the proceeds of all Bruin books will be given to the charity to help with their work.

Graham Heathfield chairman of the charity, said "most retired police dogs go on to live with their handler but some of those which do not make it as police dogs are adopted by other families, such as the Wilkies who gave Bruin a safe and loving home.

And while there is no guarantee that the dogs will have adventures like Bruin's all will make very special pets!"

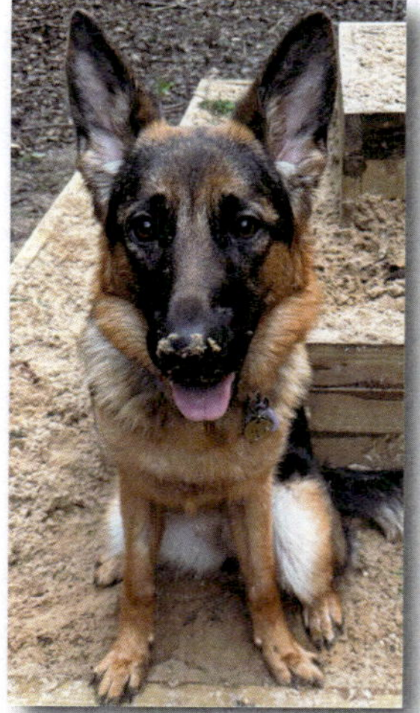

For more information you can check the WAGS website on

wagsretiredpolicedogs.co.uk

or the National Federation for Retired Service Animals, which looks after dogs from the police, fire service, prison service or border force, on:

nfrsa.org.uk.

Alternatively contact your local police dog handling team.

Book Four in the Adventures of Bruin series is Bruin and the Flytippers! which is available through Amazon or direct from the author (signed if required) at:

bruinstories@gmail.com

Photography © Charlie Hudson: Nala

How can you support Retired Police Dogs?

PC Robin Dimond has been a police Dog Handler, for the past 16 years. He spent 15 of those as a Dog Handler recently moving into the training team.

His role consists of bringing on new potential police dogs for the first year of their lives until they are old enough to complete an Initial Police Dog Course.

He trains both General Purpose Police dogs and specialist Search Explosive dogs.

Chris Davis has been a police officer for 24 years. A dog handler for the past 14 years.

He handles a German Shepherd called Wilson, who is a 7 year old Firearm Support dog and Rocky (Spaniel) a 7 year old specialist drug/cash/firearm recovery dog.

Both Chris and Rob operate within the Dog Support Unit of Hampshire and Isle of Wight Constabulary.

The Hants charity set up and run by some of the current and retired handlers is: **Pension4Paws.**

They support retired Police dogs with vet bills and rehoming etc.

https://pensions4paws.com/

Photography © Dave Pimbbet

PALM BEACH
POLICE
Photography © Dave Pimbblet

Illustration © Claire S Bicknell

Can you create a colourful
Circus of your own?

Illustration © Claire S Bicknell

Illustrations © Claire S Bicknell

Colouring Fun...

... Previously Book 1

Bruïn

• TO THE RESCUE •

By Michael Fleet

Illustrations by
Claire S Bicknell

... Previously Book 2

Brüin

& THE BURIED TREASURE

By Michael Fleet

Illustrations by
Claire S Bicknell

... Coming soon Book 4

Bruïn

& THE FLYTIPPERS

By Michael Fleet

Illustrations by
Claire S Bicknell